Mille et un points

Harrap's French Grammar Revision

Neil Creighton

NEW EDITION

Harrap London

First published in Great Britain 1978 by Portrea Publications
This edition published in Great Britain 1981
by HARRAP LIMITED
19–23 Ludgate Hill, London EC4M 7PD
Reprinted: 1981; 1982; 1983

ISBN 0 245-53776-7 (net edition)
0 245-53777-5 (not-net edition)

Printed in Great Britain by
Biddles Ltd, Guildford, Surrey

FOREWORD

Mille et Un Points was written to satisfy two specific needs — namely to imbue first examination students with a sound knowledge of French grammar, and to act as a reference handbook for more advanced students.

The author has spent many years teaching examination French at various grammar schools, and latterly in the capacity of Head of the French Department in a large comprehensive school. It is his contention that examination failure — whether at CSE, 16 +, Ordinary or Advanced levels — is frequently attributable to an ignorance of basic French structures. To remedy this deficiency, he devised, over the years, a system of grammar-revision notes; they are comprehensible and palatable to students of French and geared to their examination requirements.

Mille et Un Points has evolved from this system of grammar notes and now fills the gap in the existing market; the so-called 'Traditional' textbooks are by no means comprehensive, nor do they fully revise those (forgotten!) structures supposedly assimilated in years 1 — 4. On the other hand the purely Audio/Visual/Lingual courses often leave all but the outstanding pupils ill-equipped to handle written examinations competently and confidently.

How does *Mille et Un Points* clarify French ? It is a cross-referenced compendium of grammar which elucidates the foundations and superstructure of the French Language so essential for examination success; comprehensiveness is ensured by attention to detail, and simplicity by full exemplification of all points. A Table of Contents and an exhaustive Index ensure ease of reference, and the novel, schematic presentation with meaningful tables and copious examples of patterns provides tangibility for the student. In short, completeness and accessibility lend the book a wide range of application for first examinations and beyond.

The book is systematized as follows:

Part I - **The Ten Tenses:** a tense by tense analysis, covering meanings, formation, irregularities and usage.

Part II - **Pronouns and Adjectives:** a detailed exposition outlining the forms and usage of pronouns and corresponding adjectives.

Part III - **1001 Points Alphabetically:** an 'A - Z' codification of grammar points.

CONTENTS

Command

PART ONE - THE TEN TENSES

§1. THE PRESENT TENSE

I Meaning: Je porte = I carry, I do carry, I am carrying

II Formation

1. Regular verbs

(a) - er type, porter = to carry
Remove the - **er**, add the endings:

	Je port	**e**
	Tu port	**es**
(Elle)	Il port	**e**
	Nous port	**ons**
	Vous port	**ez**
(Elles)	Ils port	**ent**

(b) -ir type, finir = to finish
Remove the **-ir**, add the endings:

	Je fin	**is**
	Tu fin	**is**
(Elle)	Il fin	**it**
	Nous fin	**issons**
	Vous fin	**issez**
(Elles)	Ils fin	**issent**

(c) - re type, vendre = to sell
Remove the - **re**, add the endings:

subject pronouns	stem	endings
Je	vend	**s**
Tu	vend	**s**
(Elle) Il	vend	
Nous	vend	**ons**
Vous	vend	**ez**
(Elles) Ils	vend	**ent**

2. 50 Irregular verbs

		1. AVOIR *to have*	2. ÊTRE *to be*	3. ALLER *to go*	4. S'ASSEOIR *to sit down*
(J')	Je	ai	suis	vais	m' assieds
	Tu	as	es	vas	t' assieds
(Elle)	Il	a	est	va	s' assied
	Nous	avons	sommes	allons	nous asseyons
	Vous	avez	êtes	allez	vous asseyez
(Elles)	Ils	ont	sont	vont	s' asseyent

		5. BATTRE *to beat*	6. BOIRE *to drink*	7. CONDUIRE *to drive/lead*	8. CONNAÎTRE *to know (person (place*
	Je	bats	bois	conduis	connais
	Tu	bats	bois	conduis	connais
(Elle)	Il	bat	boit	conduit	connaît
	Nous	battons	buvons	conduisons	connaissons
	Vous	battez	buvez	conduisez	connaissez
(Elles)	Ils	battent	boivent	conduisent	connaissent

1

		9. COURIR *to run*	10. CRAINDRE *to fear*	11. CROIRE *to believe/ think*	12. CROÎTRE *to grow*
	Je	cours	crains	crois	croîs
	Tu	cours	crains	crois	croîs
(Elle)	Il	court	craint	croit	croît
	Nous	courons	craignons	croyons	croissons
	Vous	courez	craignez	croyez	croissez
(Elles)	Ils	courent	craignent	croient	croissent

		13. CUEILLIR *to gather*	14. DEVOIR *to owe/ have to*	15. DIRE *to say/tell*	16. DORMIR *to sleep*
	Je	cueille	dois	dis	dors
	Tu	cueilles	dois	dis	dors
(Elle)	Il	cueille	doit	dit	dort
	Nous	cueillons	devons	disons	dormons
	Vous	cueillez	devez	**dites**	dormez
(Elles)	Ils	cueillent	doivent	disent	dorment

		17. ÉCRIRE *to write*	18. FAIRE *to do/make*	19. FUIR *to flee*	20. HAÏR *to hate*
(J')	Je	écris	fais	fuis	hais
	Tu	écris	fais	fuis	hais
(Elle)	Il	écrit	fait	fuit	hait
	Nous	écrivons	faisons	fuyons	haïssons
	Vous	écrivez	**faites**	fuyez	haïssez
(Elles)	Ils	écrivent	font	fuient	haïssent

		21. LIRE *to read*	22. METTRE *to put*	23. MOURIR *to die*	24. NAÎTRE *to be born*
	Je	lis	mets	meurs	nais
	Tu	lis	mets	meurs	nais
(Elle)	Il	lit	met	meurt	naît
	Nous	lisons	mettons	mourons	naissons
	Vous	lisez	mettez	mourez	naissez
(Elles)	Ils	lisent	mettent	meurent	naissent

		25. NUIRE *to harm*	26. OUVRIR *to open*	27. PARTIR *to depart*	28. PLAIRE *to please*
(J')	Je	nuis	ouvre	pars	plais
	Tu	nuis	ouvres	pars	plais
(Elle)	Il	nuit	ouvre	part	plaît
	Nous	nuisons	ouvrons	partons	plaisons
	Vous	nuisez	ouvrez	partez	plaisez
(Elles)	Ils	nuisent	ouvrent	partent	plaisent

		29. POUVOIR *to be able*	30. PRENDRE *to take*	31. RECEVOIR *to receive*	32. RIRE *to laugh*
	Je	peux (puis-je ?)	prends	reçois	ris
	Tu	peux	prends	reçois	ris
(Elle)	Il	peut	prend	reçoit	rit
	Nous	pouvons	prenons	recevons	rions
	Vous	**pouvez**	prenez	recevez	riez
(Elles)	Ils	peuvent	prennent	reçoivent	rient

		33. ROMPRE *to break*	34. SAVOIR *to know (facts)*	35. SENTIR. *to feel/smell*	36. SERVIR *to serve*
	Je	romps	sais	sens	sers
	Tu	romps	sais	sens	sers
(Elle)	Il	rompt	sait	sent	sert
	Nous	rompons	savons	sentons	servons
	Vous	rompez	savez	sentez	servez
(Elles)	Ils	rompent	savent	sentent	servent

		37. SORTIR *to go/come out*	38. SUFFIRE *to suffice*	39. SUIVRE *to follow*	40. SE TAIRE *to be silent*
	Je	sors	suffis	suis	me tais
	Tu	sors	suffis	suis	te tais
(Elle)	Il	sort	suffit	suit	se tait
	Nous	sortons	suffisons	suivons	nous taisons
	Vous	sortez	suffisez	suivez	vous taisez
(Elles)	Ils	sortent	suffisent	suivent	se taisent

		41. TENIR *to hold*	42. VAINCRE *to vanquish*	43. VALOIR *to be worth*	44. VENIR *to come*
	Je	tiens	vaincs	vaux	viens
	Tu	tiens	vaincs	vaux	viens
(Elle)	Il	tient	vainc	vaut	vient
	Nous	tenons	vainquons	valons	venons
	Vous	tenez	vainquez	valez	venez
(Elles)	Ils	tiennent	vainquent	valent	viennent

		45. VÊTIR *to clothe*	46. VIVRE *to live*	47. VOIR *to see*	48. VOULOIR *to wish/want*
	Je	vêts	vis	vois	veux
	Tu	vêts	vis	vois	veux
(Elle)	Il	vêt	vit	voit	veut
	Nous	vêtons	vivons	voyons	voulons
	Vous	vêtez	vivez	voyez	voulez
(Elles)	Ils	vêtent	vivent	voient	veulent

		49. FALLOIR *to be necessary*	50. PLEUVOIR *to rain*
	Il	Il faut	Il pleut

Some COMPOUNDS based on the Irregular Verbs:

BATTRE	combattre	= to combat	abattre	= to knock down
	se battre	= to fight		
CONDUIRE	construire	= to build	détruire	= to destroy
	instruire	= to instruct	traduire	= to translate
	produire	= to produce		
CONNAÎTRE	reconnaître	= to recognize	paraître	= to seem
	disparaître	= to disappear	apparaître	= to appear

COURIR	accourir	=	to run up to			
CRAINDRE	plaindre	=	to pity	se plaindre	=	to complain
	att*EI*ndre	=	to reach	j*OI*ndre	=	to join
CROÎTRE	accroître	=	to increase			
CUEILLIR	accueillir	=	to welcome			
ÉCRIRE	décrire	=	to describe	s'inscrire	=	to register/book in
METTRE	commettre	=	to commit	omettre	=	to omit
	promettre	=	to promise	permettre	=	to permit
OUVRIR	couvrir	=	to cover	découvrir	=	to discover/uncover
	offrir	=	to offer	souffrir	=	to suffer
PRENDRE	apprendre	=	to learn	comprendre	=	to understand
	surprendre	=	to surprise			
RECEVOIR	apercevoir	=	to notice	concevoir	=	to conceive
RIRE	sourire	=	to smile			
ROMPRE	corrompre	=	to corrupt	interrompre	=	to interupt
SENTIR	mentir	=	to lie			
SUIVRE	poursuivre	=	to pursue			
TENIR	contenir	=	to contain	soutenir	=	to support
	obtenir	=	to obtain	retenir	=	to keep
	appartenir	=	to belong	maintenir	=	to maintain
VAINCRE	convaincre	=	to convince			
VENIR	devenir	=	to become	parvenir (à)	=	to succeed/manage
	convenir	=	to suit/fit	se souvenir de	=	to remember
VIVRE	survivre	=	to survive			

3. –ER VERBS WITH PECULIARITIES IN THE PRESENT TENSE

(a) –CER verbs:
        Before o the c takes a *cédille* (ﻭ)
    Commencer = to begin
        Je   commence
        Tu   commences   *Also:* avancer = to advance
        Il   commence   lancer = to launch, to hurl
        Nous commenÇons   menacer = to threaten
        Vous commencez   agacer = to annoy
        Ils   commencent

    Note: The (ﻭ) is used before a and u in other tenses:
            Imperfect: je commenÇais,   **Perfect:** j'ai aperÇu
                Past Historic: il avanÇa

(b) –GER verbs:
        Before o the g is *cushioned* with an E
    Manger = to eat
        Je   mange
        Tu   manges   *Also:* se diriger vers = to go towards
        Il   mange   nager = to swim
        Nous mangEons   partager = to divide out/share
        Vous mangez   dégager = to release
        Ils   mangent   encourager = to encourage

    Note: The **E** is placed before the a in other tenses:
            Imperfect: ils nagEaient,   **Past Historic:** il mangEa

(c) Appeler and jeter:
The consonant is **doubled** before the silent endings.
The **nous** and **vous** form stems remain as in the Infinitive.

		Appeler = to call	**Jeter** = to throw
(Je)	J'	appe**LL**e	je**TT**e
	Tu	appe**LL**es	je**TT**es
(Elle) Il		appe**LL**e	je**TT**e
Nous		appelons	jetons
Vous		appelez	jetez
(Elles) Ils		appe**LL**ent	je**TT**ent

Also: se rappeler = to remember

(d) Verbs taking a Grave Accent (è) before silent endings
The **nous** and **vous** form stems remain as in the Infinitive.

	Acheter *to buy*	**Mener** *to lead*	**Lever** *to raise*	**Espérer** *to hope*	**Céder** *to yield*	**Répéter** *to repeat*	**Préférer** *to prefer*
J'	achète	mène	lève	espère	cède	ré pète	pré fère
Tu	achètes	mènes	lèves	espères	cèdes	ré pètes	pré fères
Il	achète	mène	lève	espère	cède	ré pète	pré fère
Nous	achetons	menons	levons	espérons	cédons	ré pétons	pré férons
Vous	achetez	menez	levez	espérez	cédez	ré pétez	pré férez
Ils	achètent	mènent	lèvent	espèrent	cèdent	ré pètent	pré fèrent

Also: geler - to freeze, régner - to reign, pénétrer - to penetrate/enter.

Note: These Future and Conditional stems take a grave accent:
j'achèterai, je mènerais, je lèverai, il gèlerait.

(e) - oyer and - uyer verbs:
Before silent endings **y** becomes **i**

	Essuyer *to wipe*	**Nettoyer** *to clean*
J'	essu**i**e	netto**i**e
Tu	essu**i**es	netto**i**es
Il	essu**i**e	netto**i**e
Nous	essuyons	nettoyons
Vous	essuyez	nettoyez
Ils	essu**i**ent	netto**i**ent

Also: ennuyer - to annoy
employer - to use
envoyer - to send

Note: The Future and Conditional stems: j'essu**i**erai, je netto**i**erai.
(Remember the irregular Future of envoyer, j'**enverrai**.)

(f) - ayer verbs: The change to **i** is optional:

	Payer *to pay*				**Essayer** *to try*		
Je	paye	)	(pa**i**e		essaye	)	(essa**i**e
Tu	payes	)	(pa**i**es		essayes	)	(essa**i**es
Il	paye	)	(pa**i**e		essaye	)	(essa**i**e
Nous	payons	)OR(payons		essayons	) OR (essayons		
Vous	payez	)	(payez		essayez	)	(essayez
Ils	payent	)	(pa**i**ent		essayent	)	(essa**i**ent

§2. THE FUTURE TENSE

A. THE TRUE FUTURE

I. Meaning: I **shall/will** carry   (See also Section 55, Quand)

II. Formation: Stem + Ending

1. - er verbs		STEM	ENDING			AUXIL VERB	
e.g. porter,	Je	porter	AI		I	shall	carry
donner: use	Tu	porter	AS		You	will	carry
Infinitive as the	(Elle) Il	porter	A	(She) He		will	carry
Stem	Nous	porter	ONS		We	shall	carry
	Vous	porter	EZ		You	will	carry
	(Elles) Ils	porter	ONT		They	will	carry
2. - ir verbs							
e.g. finir,choisir,	Je	finir	AI		I	shall	finish
remplir: use	Tu	finir	AS		You	will	finish
Infinitive as the	(Elle) Il	finir	A	(She) He		will	finish
Stem	Nous	finir	ONS		We	shall	finish
	Vous	finir	EZ		You	will	finish
	(Elles) Ils	finir	ONT		They	will	finish
3. - re verbs							
e.g. vendre,	Je	vendr	AI		I	shall	sell
entendre: remove	Tu	vendr	AS		You	will	sell
final E from the	(Elle) Il	vendr	A	(She) He		will	sell
Infinitive and	Nous	vendr	ONS		We	shall	sell
use as the **Stem**	Vous	vendr	EZ		You	will	sell
	(Elles) Ils	vendr	ONT		They	will	sell

4. Irregular Futures

Many Irregular Verbs take their Future Stems from the infinitive:

partir   je **partir** ...   ai = I shall depart
             ..*or*, if the Irregular Verb ends in **-re**, remove the **- e**:

boire   je **boir** ....   ai = I shall drink
croître   je **croîtr** ..   ai = I shall grow

HOWEVER, THESE EXCEPTIONAL STEMS MUST BE LEARNED | **COMPOUNDS**

avoir	j' **aur**...	ai = I shall have		
être	je **ser** ...	ai = I shall be		
aller	j' **ir**....	ai = I shall go	m'en ir . . . . ai	
s'asseoir je m'	**assiér**....	ai = I shall sit down		
courir	je **courr**....	ai = I shall run	accourr. . . . ai	
cueillir	je **cueiller**...	ai = I shall gather	accueill*er* . . ai	
devoir	je **devr**...	ai = I shall have to/owe		
envoyer	j' **enverr**...	ai = I shall send		
faire	je **fer**....	ai = I shall do/make		
falloir	il **faudr**...	a = It will be necessary		
mourir	je **mourr**....	ai = I shall die		
pleuvoir	il **pleuvr**...	a = It will rain		
pouvoir	je **pourr**....	ai = I shall be able		

recevoir	je **recevr..**	ai =	I shall receive	apercevr.....ai	
savoir	je **saur...**	ai =	I shall know (facts)		
tenir	je **tiendr..**	ai =	I shall hold		
valoir	je **vaudr...**	ai =	I shall be worth		
venir	je **viendr...**	ai =	I shall come	reviendr.....ai	
				deviendr.... ai	
voir	je **verr...**	ai =	I shall see	reverr........ ai	
vouloir	je **voudr...**	ai =	I shall wish/want		

5. - ER verbs with peculiarities

appeler	j' **appeller...**	ai)	**Consonant is Doubled**
jeter	je **jetter.....**	ai)	
acheter	j' **achèter....**	ai)	**Take a Grave Accent (`)**
mener	je **mèner.....**	ai)	
lever	je **lèver....**	ai)	
essuyer	j' **essuier...**	ai)	**y becomes i**
ennuyer	j' **ennuier...**	ai)	
nettoyer	je **nettoier...**	ai)	
payer	je **payerai or paierai)**		**The change to i is optional**
essayer	j' **(essayer..**	ai)	
	(essaier..	ai)	

B. THE IMMEDIATE FUTURE

I. Meaning: I *am going* to carry

II. Formation: (Aller)
(to go) **+ Infinitive**

	ALLER + INFINITIVE			TO GO +	INFINITIVE
Je	**vais**	porter	I	am going	to carry
Tu	**vas**	finir	You	are going	to finish
(Elle) Il	**va**	vendre	She/He	is going	to sell
Nous	**allons**	nager	We	are going	to swim
Vous	**allez**	faire	You	are going	to do/make
(Elles) Ils	**vont**	voir	They	are going	to see

Note: être sur le point de = to be about to
Je suis sur le point de sortir = I am about to go out

§3. THE CONDITIONAL TENSE

1. Meaning: I **would** carry. (See Section 58, Si and its meanings)

II. Formation: Future Stem + Imperfect endings.

FUTURE STEMS +	ENDINGS			AUXILIARY VERB	
Je porter	**ais**	=	I	WOULD	carry
Tu finir	**ais**	=	You	WOULD	finish
(Elle) Il vendr	**ait**	=	She / He	WOULD	sell
Nous saur	**ions**	=	We	WOULD	know (a fact)
Vous verr	**iez**	=	You	WOULD	see
(Elles) Ils jetter	**aient**	=	They	WOULD	throw

Note 1: In the first persons singular and plural, ' I should....' and ' We should...' are more proper in English. However, do not confuse this with the 'should' of DEVOIR (**ought to**) (Section 33)

Note 2: ' Would' can sometimes indicate an Imperfect Tense - when it really means 'used to' ' Every morning, I would (= used to) get up at 8 o'clock....'

§4. THE IMPERFECT TENSE

I. Meanings

1. Recognition

(a)   ...WAS ....ING   I WAS givING

...WERE....ING   We WERE givING

As I WAS walkING down the road......
As we WERE walkING down the road.....

(b)   ...USED TO...   I USED TO give

Every day I USED TO visit my grandfather

(c).... WOULD ...... (when = USED TO....)   I WOULD give

Every week I WOULD   visit my grandfather
(*Would* normally indicates the **Conditional Tense**)

(d) THE SIMPLE PAST - DISGUISED   I gave

Apply the TEST - if (a), (b) or (c) can be inserted, then the 'simple past' is a **Disguised Imperfect**

As I WALKED down the road
(Test: really means **WAS** walkING ∴Imperfect)

Every week I VISITED my grandfather.
(Test: really means **USED TO** or **WOULD** ∴ Imperfect)

2. Examples of the Imperfect

(a) Description or State

	The SIMPLE PAST or DISGUISED IMPERFECT
Elle **portait** une robe bleue = She was wearing a blue dress	She *wore*
Nous **étions** heureux = We were happy	

(b) Repetition or Habit

Tous les matins elle **se levait** à huit heures puis elle **lisait** le journal = Every morning she used to get up at 8 o'clock then she would read the newspaper	She *got up* She *read*

(c) Continuous Background

Nous **mangions**...	(quand il est arrivé (quand il arriva	
We were eating...	*when he arrived*	
Pendant qu'elle **chantait** ...	(elle est tombée (elle tomba	While she *sang*
While she was singing...	*she fell*	
Comme il **regardait**...	(elle l'a giflé (elle le gifla	As he *watched*
As he was watching...	*she slapped him*	

Continuous Background: Imperfect →	*Interrupted by a sudden action: Perfect or Past Historic* ↓

II. Formation

1. Regular verbs

(a) Take the **nous** form of the **Present Tense**:

nous donnons (-er) nous finissons (- ir) nous vendons (-re)

(b) Remove the - **ons** to obtain the **Stem**:

nous **donn** (ons) nous **finiss** (ons) nous **vend** (ons)

(c) Add the following ENDINGS:

Je	donn	**AIS**	finiss	**AIS**	vend	**AIS**
Tu	donn	**AIS**	finiss	**AIS**	vend	**AIS**
(Elle) Il	donn	**AIT**	finiss	**AIT**	vend	**AIT**
Nous	donn	**IONS**	finiss	**IONS**	vend	**IONS**
Vous	donn	**IEZ**	finiss	**IEZ**	vend	**IEZ**
(Elles)Ils	donn	**AIENT**	finiss	**AIENT**	vend	**AIENT**

2. Verbs Irregular in the Present Tense: Same Formation Procedure

(a) Take the **nous** form of the **Irregular Present Tense**

nous buvons, nous rions, nous avons, nous voyons, nous écrivons

(b) Remove the - **ons** to obtain the **Stem**

(c) Add the endings:

		buv		ri		
	Je	buv	**AIS**	ri	**AIS**	
	Tu	buv	**AIS**	ri	**AIS**	
(Elle)	Il	buv	**AIT**	ri	**AIT**	
	Nous	buv	**IONS**	ri	**IONS**)
	Vous	buv	**IEZ**	ri	**IEZ**)	Note the double I
(Elles)	Ils	buv	**AIENT**	ri	**AIENT**	

3. Être is an exception - the Stem is ÉT--------

J'	**ÉT**ais	Nous	**ÉT**ions
Tu	**ÉT**ais	Vous	**ÉT**iez
(Elle) Il	**ÉT**ait	(Elles) Ils	**ÉT**aient

Note: the impersonal verbs *pleuvoir* and *falloir*, for which there is no *nous* form:

PRESENT	**IMPERFECT**
il faut	il fallait = it was necessary
il pleut	il pleuvait = it was raining

4. Other Irregularities

    (a)   *g* cushioned by **E** before *a:* je mangEais, ils nagEaient,etc

    (b)   *c* softened by (ç) before *a:* il commenÇait, ils avanÇaient, etc.

    BUT nous mang**ions**, vous commenc**iez**, as normal (See Section 20)

§5. THE PAST HISTORIC TENSE (PAST DEFINITE)

I. Meaning

1. Simple Narrative

Hier, Jean **se leva, sortit,**puis il **acheta** un journal.
Yesterday John got up, went out,then he bought a newspaper.

Note the Imperfect - for Repetition or Habit.

Tous les matins, Jean se lev*ait*, sort*ait* puis il achet*ait* un journal.
Every morning, John used to get up, used to go out then he used to buy
a newspaper.

2. Completed Past Events

Past Historic Event	Note the Imperfect
Jean ferma la porte	parce qu'il avait froid.....**Description or State.**
Jean ferma la porte	qui était ouverte.............**Description or State.**
Jean ferma la porte	pendant qu'il parlait.......**Continuous Background**

Note: The Past Historic Tense is confined to written French—
NOT to be used in conversation or Direct Speech.

II. Formation - Four Types

1. - AI type for - ER verbs (including ALLER)

Add the following ENDINGS to the STEM

Je   donnai   = I gave
Tu   donnas   etc.
(Elle) Il   donna
Nous donnâmes
Vous donnâtes
(Elles)Ils donnèrent

2. - IS Types.

(a) for - IR verbs, add these ENDINGS to the STEM

Je   finis *- I finished
Tu finis *   etc.
(Elle) Il finit *
Nous finîmes
Vous finîtes
(Elles) Ils finirent

(b) for - RE verbs, add these ENDINGS to the STEM

Je   vendis - I sold
Tu vendis   etc.
(Elle) Il vendit
Nous vendîmes
Vous vendîtes
(Elles)Ils vendirent

(* a form identical to the Present Tense)

(c) for certain Irregular verbs

acquérir	to acquire	j'acquis	naître	to be born	je naquis
s'asseoir	to sit down	je m'assis	nuire	to harm	je nuisis
battre	to beat	je battis	ouvrir	to open	j'ouvris
conduire	to drive	je conduisis	partir	to leave	je partis
craindre	to fear	je craignis	prendre	to take	je pris
joindre	to join	je joignis	rire	to laugh	je ris
atteindre	to reach	j'atteignis	rompre	to break	je rompis
cueillir	to gather	je cueillis	sentir	to feel	je sentis
dire	to say/tell	je dis	servir	to serve	je servis
dormir	to sleep	je dormis	sortir	to go out	je sortis
écrire	to write	j'écrivis	suffire	to suffice	je suffis
faire	to do/make	je fis	suivre	to follow	je suivis
fuire	to flee	je fuis	vaincre	to conquer	je vainquis
haïr	to hate	je haïs	vêtir	to clothe	je vêtis
mettre	to put	je mis	voir	to see	je vis

3. - US type, for other Irregular Verbs

	Je	bus	I drank
	Tu	bus	etc.
(Elle)	Il	but	
	Nous	bûmes	
	Vous	bûtes	
(Elles)Ils		burent	

avoir	to have	j'eus	mourir	to die	je mourus
être	to be	je fus	plaire	to please	je plus
boire	to drink	je bus	pleuvoir	to rain	il plut
conclure	to conclude	je conclus	pouvoir	to be able	je pus
connaître	to know (pers)	je connus	recevoir	to receive	je reçus
courir	to run	je courus	résoudre	to resolve	je résolus
croire	to believe	je crus	savoir	to know(fact)	je sus
croître	to grow	je crûs	se taire	to be silent	je me tus
devoir	to owe/must	je dus	valoir	to be worth	je valus
falloir	to be necess.	il fallut	vivre	to live	je vécus
lire	to read	je lus	vouloir	to wish/want	je voulus

4. - INS Exceptions - Venir, Tenir and Compounds.

	VENIR			**TENIR**	
	Je	vins - I came		Je	tins - I held
	Tu	vins etc.		Tu	tins etc.
(Elle) Il	vint		(Elle)Il	tint	
	Nous vînmes			Nous tînmes	
	Vous vîntes			Vous tîntes	
(Elles) Ils	vinrent		(Elles)Ils	tinrent	

Note: Compound Verbs are based on many of the Irregular Past Historics:

Je mis..... Je commis)
Je reçus.. J'aperçus)   See list of Compounds (Sec. 1 Present Tense)
Je tins.... Je retins   )

THE FIVE COMPOUND TENSES §6 — §10

§6. THE PERFECT TENSE

A. AVOIR TYPE

I. Meanings ———————————→

II.Formation - Avoir + Past Part.

			HAVE/HAS	SIMPLE PAST
J'	ai	gagné	I have won	I won
	Tu as	mangé	You have eaten	You ate
(Elle)	Il a	vendu	(She) He has sold	(She) He sold
	Nous avons	bu	We have drunk	We drank
	Vous avez	pris	You have taken	You took
(Elles) Ils	ont	vaincu	They have conquered	They conquered

III. Agreements.

  1. with preceding DIRECT objects

  (a) Object Pronouns (from the Football Team - Sec.11, Object Pronouns)

      Où est la pomme ? - Je **L'** ai mangé**E**...............(F.S.)

      Où sont les assiettes ? - Je **LES** ai cassé**ES**........(F.P.)

      Où est le livre ? - Je **L'**ai vu.............................(M.S.)

      Où sont les journaux ? - Il **LES** a perdu**S**..........(M.P.)

NOTE:	
M =	Masculine
F =	Feminine
S =	Singular
P =	Plural

  (b) Quel as a signpost

      Quelle robe as-tu acheté**E**...............(F.S.)

      Quelles assiettes a-t-il cassé**ES** ?.......(F.P.)

      Quel canif as-tu vu ?.....................(M.S.)

      Quels livres as-tu lu**S** ?.....................(M.P.)

  (c) QUE as a signpost

      Voilà la voiture **que** j'ai acheté**E**.............**(F.S.)**

      Voilà les règles **que** j'ai trouvé**ES**.....(F.P.)

      Voici le livre **que** j'ai lu...................(M.S.)

      Où sont les ânes **que** tu as vendu**S** ? (M.P.)

  (d) Combien as a signpost

      Combien de lettres as-tu écrit**ES** ?....(F.P.)

      Combien de livres avez-vous lu**S** ?.....(M.P.)

2. Non-Agreements

    (a) EN - of it, of them, some, any.

    As-tu mangé des pommes ? - Oui, j'**en** ai mangé   trois

    Have you eaten any of the apples ? Yes, I've eaten three *of them*

    (b) preceding INdirect Object Pronouns - e.g. LUI and LEUR

    Nous **leur** avons donné_ *la viande*

        └─IND OBJ ─┘ *(Direct Object, but not Preceding)*

    We have given (to) them the meat

IV. Verbs taking Avoir:

    The vast majority of verbs, *except* **(The 16,** taking être

                                 (Reflexives, taking être

B. ÊTRE TYPE

I. Meanings ────────────→

II. Formation - Être + Past Part.

			HAVE/HAS	SIMPLE PAST
Je	suis	allé (E)	I have gone	I went
Tu	es	arrivé (E)	You have arrived	You arrived
Il	est	parti.	He has left	He left
Elle	est	partiE	She has left	She left
Nous	sommes	venu (E)S	We have come	We came
Vous	êtes	rentre (E) (S)	You have gone home	You went home
Ils	sont	néS	They have been born	They were born
Elles	sont	néES	They have been born	They were born

III. Agreements

1. With the Subject

Je	suis	venu.....(M.S.)	**Vous**	êtes	entréE...... (F.S.)	
Je	suis	venuE...(F.S.)				
			Vous	êtes	entréES....(F.P.)	
Tu	es	sorti_....(M.S.)	Vous	êtes	entré_........(M.S.)	
Tu	es	sortiE..(F.S.)	Vous	êtes	entréS......(M.P.)	
Il	est	revenu_(M.S.)	Ils	sont	tombéS...(M.P.)	
Elle	est	revenuE..(F.S.)	Elles	sont	tombéES.(F.P.)	
Nous	sommes	alléS......(M.P.)				
Nous	sommes	alléES...(F.P.)				

2. Non-Agreement of certain ' Être Verbs ' when they have their own Direct Object (That is, they are transitive)

Sortir = to take out   Descendre = to get down
Rentrer = to bring in   Monter = to take up/go up

(a) These verbs now take avoir : (* indicates a direct object)

E.g: Il a sorti *son argent* *   He has taken out his money
     Elle a descendu *les valises* *   She has brought down the suitcases
     Elle a monté *l'escalier* *   She has gone up the stairs
     (Contrast: Elle est montéE vite = She has gone up quickly)

       Il a rentré *les outils* *   He has brought in the tools

(b) Past Participle now agrees with any Preceding Direct Object

E.g: **Quelles** valises as-tu montéES.........(F.P.)

IV. Verbs taking ÊTRE   - The 16   - (And all Reflexive verbs)

(aller	to go	allé	gone
(venir	to come	venu	come
(arriver	to arrive	arrivé	arrived
(partir	to leave	parti	left
(entrer	to go in	entré	gone in
(sortir	to go out	sorti	gone out

(rester	to remain	resté	remained
(retourner	to return	retourné	returned
(descendre	to go down	descendu	gone down
(monter	to go up	monté	gone up
(naître	to be born	né	been born
(mourir	to die	mort	died
(tomber	to fall	tombé	fallen

Compounds	(revenir	to come back	revenu	come back
	(devenir	to become	devenu	become
	(rentrer	to go home	rentré	gone home

C. REFLEXIVE TYPE

I. Meanings ────────────────→

II. Formation - **Reflexive Pronoun +**
            Être + Past Part.

				HAVE/HAS	SIMPLE PAST
Je	me	suis	réveillé **(E)**	I have woken up	I woke up
Tu	t'	es	reposé **(E)**	You have rested	You rested
Il	s'	est	arrêté_	He has stopped	He stopped
Elle	s'	est	levé**E**	She has got up	She got up
Nous	nous	sommes	caché **(E)S**	We have hidden	We hid
Vous	vous	êtes	lavé **(E) (S)**	You have washed	You washed
Ils	se	sont	trompé**S**	They have been wrong	They were wrong
Elles	se	sont	dépêché**ES**	They have hurried	They hurried

III. Agreements

1. **With the Reflexive Pronoun** - which is the Preceding Direct Object in most cases.

Il **S**'est reposé_	(M.S.)
Elle **S**'est reposé**E**	(F.S.)
Nous **NOUS** sommes caché**S**	(M.P.)
Elles **SE** sont arrêté**ES**	(F.P.)

2. **Non-Agreement** - when the Reflexive Pronoun is an **IN**direct Object.

E.g: Elles **SE** sont écrit_ des lettres

They wrote letters TO each other

Elle **S**'est acheté une maison

She bought a house (*for* herself)

| **SE** is an **IN**direct Object in these cases |
| Des lettres, une maison, and le visage |
| are Direct Objects. |

Elle s'est lavé le visage
(*Contrast:* Elle s'est lavé**E**)

IV. ALL REFLEXIVE VERBS take ÊTRE

THE REMAINING COMPOUND TENSES

Formation Principles:
> **auxiliary verb** *in the appropriate tense* + **past participle**
> (include the **Reflexive Pronoun** in the Reflexive type)

Agreement Principles:
> similar to the **Perfect Tense: avoir type**, Page 13; **être type**, Page 14;
> **Reflexive type**, Page 15.

§7. THE PLUPERFECT   (. . . had . . .)

Put the auxiliary into the Imperfect Tense.
A. AVOIR Type:	J' **avais** mangé	I HAD eaten
B. ÊTRE Type:	J' **étais** arrivé	I HAD arrived
C. REFLEXIVE:	Je m' **étais** levé	I HAD got up

§8. THE FUTURE PERFECT   (. . .shall/will have. . .)

Put the auxiliary into the Future Tense.
A. AVOIR Type:	Elle **aura** mangé	She WILL HAVE eaten
B. ÊTRE Type:	Elle **sera** arrivéE	She WILL HAVE arrived
C. REFLEXIVE:	Ils se **seront** levéS	They WILL HAVE got up

§9. THE CONDITIONAL PERFECT   (. . . should/would have. .)

Put the auxiliary into the Conditional Tense.
A. AVOIR Type:	J' **aurais** mangé	I WOULD HAVE eaten
B. ÊTRE Type:	Je **serais** arrivé	I WOULD HAVE arrived
C. REFLEXIVE:	Il se **serait** levé	He WOULD HAVE got up

§10. THE PAST ANTERIOR   (. . . had . . .)

Put the auxiliary into the Past Historic Tense
A. AVOIR Type:	J' **eus** mangé	I HAD eaten
B. ÊTRE Type:	Je **fus** arrivé	I HAD arrived
C. REFLEXIVE:	Il se **fut** levé	He HAD got up

Used instead of the Pluperfect in narrative, (i) *after conjunctions of time,*
e.g: quand, lorsque, aussitôt que (as soon as), dès que (as soon as), à peine
(hardly) & (ii) *when the main verb is in the Past Historic: Dès qu'il eut
mangé, il* sortit = As soon as he had eaten, he went out.

HOW TO FORM PAST PARTICIPLES

1. Regular

  - **ER verbs:**   Remove the **R** and add an acute accent (´)

> E.g: porter = porté
  - **IR verbs:**   Remove the **R**

> E.g: finir = fini

  - **RE verbs:**   Remove the **RE** and add **U**

> E.g: vendre = vendu

2. Irregular

acquérir	= to acquire	acquis	= acquired
avoir	= to have	eu	= had
être	= to be	été	= been
s'asseoir	= to sit down	assis	= sat down
battre	= to beat	battu	= beaten
boire	= to drink	bu	= drunk
conduire	= to drive/lead	conduit	= driven/led
connaître	= to know	connu	= known
coudre	= to sew	cousu	= sewn
courir	= to run	couru	= run
(craindre	= to fear	craint	= feared
(atteindre	= to reach	atteint	= reached
(joindre	= to join	joint	= joined
croire	= to believe	cru	= believed
croître	= to grow	crû	= grown
cueillir	= to gather	cueilli	= gathered
devoir	= to owe/must	dû (due)	= owed/had to
dire	= to say/tell	dit	= said/told
dormir	= to sleep	dormi	= slept
écrire	= to write	écrit	= written
faire	= to do/make	fait	= done/made
falloir	= to be necessary	fallu	= was necessary
fuire	= to flee	fui	= fled
haïr	= to hate	haï	= hated
mettre	= to put	mis	= put
moudre	= to grind	moulu	= ground
mourir	= to die	mort	– died
naître	= to be born	né	= been born/was born
nuire	= to harm	nui	= harmed
ouvrir	= to open	ouvert	= opened
paraître	= to seem	paru	= seemed
partir	= to leave	parti	= left
plaire	= to please	plu	= pleased
pleuvoir	= to rain	plu	= rained
pouvoir	= to be able	pu	= been able
prendre	= to take	pris	= taken
(recevoir	= to receive	reçu	= received
(apercevoir	= to perceive	aperçu	= perceived/noticed
résoudre	= to resolve	résolu	= resolved
rire	= to laugh	ri	= laughed
rompre	= to break	rompu	= broken
savoir	= to know	su	= known
sentir	= to feel/smell	senti	= felt/smelt
sortir	= to go/come out	sorti	= gone/come out
suffire	= to suffice	suffi	= sufficed
suivre	= to follow	suivi	= followed
se taire	= to be silent	tu	= been silent
tenir	= to hold	tenu	= held
vaincre	= to conquer	vaincu	= conquered
valoir	= to be worth	valu	= been worth/was worth
venir	= to come	venu	= come
vêtir	= to clothe	vêtu	= clothed
vivre	= to live	vécu	= lived
voir	= to see	vu	= seen
vouloir	= to wish/want	voulu	= wished/wanted

Note: Compounds are modelled on certain of above verbs

PART TWO — PRONOUNS AND ADJECTIVES

§11. OBJECT PRONOUNS

1. Meanings

PRONOUN	DIRECT OBJECT	INDIRECT OBJECT
me	me	to or for me
te	you (singular/familiar)	to (for) you
se	Used with Reflexives	
nous	us	to (for) us
vous	you (sing/polite/plu)	to (for) you
le) L' la) les	him or it (masc) her or it (fem) them (masc & fem)	
lui leur		to (for) him/her to (for) them (masc & fem)

Y (a) There

Vas-tu à la bibliothèque ? - Oui, j'**Y** vais. (I am going THERE)

(Also ' there ' with the sense of ' in it ' :

Que vois-tu dans cette armoire ? - J' **Y** vois des tasses.
= What can you see in this cupboard ? - I see some cups (IN IT))

(b) It or Them.......after verbs taking ' à '

Répondre à: Voici la dépêche ! - Répondez - **Y**
Here's the telegram ! - Answer IT

S'attendre à: Quelle explosion ! - Je m'**Y** attendais
What an explosion ! - I expected IT

(c) à + Infinitive

Peux - tu couper l'arbre ? — Oui, j'**Y** parviendrai (= à le couper)

Can you cut (down) thè tree ? — Yes, I shall manage IT

EN (a) of it

As-tu de la farine ? — J'**EN** ai beaucoup... plenty OF IT

(b) of them

Combien de frères as-tu ? — J'**EN** ai deux...two OF THEM

(c) some

As-tu du sucre ? — Oui, j'**EN** ai......SOME (of it)

(d) Any

As-tu du fromage ? — Non, je n'**EN** ai pas..ANY (of it)

(e) It or Them ... after verbs taking ' DE ':

Se souvenir de: je m'**EN** souviens = I remember **IT** or **THEM**
Se servir de: Je m'**EN** sers = I use **IT** or **THEM**

18

2. POSITION OF OBJECT PRONOUNS
(a) Immediately before the verb:

Je **le** porte = I carry it.
Nous **les** porterons = We shall carry them.
Le voici ! = Here he is !   **Te** voilà ! = There you are !

– Same with Interrogatives and Negatives:
Les voyez-vous? = Do you see them?
Il ne **nous** voit pas = He does not see us.

– Same with the Perfect and other Compound Tenses:
Je **les** ai vus = I have seen them.
Elle l'avait volé = She had stolen it.

– BUT the **Imperative Affirmative** *is the exception – Pronouns are attached with a hyphen:*
Mange-**le**!   Eat it!
Poussez-**moi**!   Push me!   (Note: *me* becomes **moi**)
Donnons-**les**!   Let's give them!

Reflexive $\begin{cases} \text{Lave-\textbf{toi}! Wash (yourself)! (Note: \textit{te} becomes \textbf{toi})} \\ \text{Lavez-\textbf{vous}! Wash (yourself/selves)!} \\ \text{Lavons-\textbf{nous}! Let us wash (ourselves)!} \end{cases}$

(The **Imperative Negative** *is normal – ne ME poussez pas! ne TE lave pas! For further details of the* **Imperative with Object Pronouns** *see section 39)*

(b) Immediately before an Infinitive:

Je vais **les** voir = I am going to see them.
J'ai décidé de **le** manger = I decided to eat it.
Avant de **les** cacher = Before hiding them.
Après **les** avoir trouvés = After having found them.

3. ORDER OF PRONOUNS if TWO occur.

Question: When there are two Object Pronouns to be translated into French which of the two goes first ?
Answer: The order is governed by the *numbered columns* in the *football team* below:

ME TE SE NOUS VOUS	LE LA LES	LUI LEUR	Y	EN
(1)	(2)	(3)	(4)	(5)

He gives IT TO ME.......... Il **me le** donne
      (2)   (1)   (1)(2)
They give (TO) HIM THEM...Ils **les lui** donnent
        (3)   (2)   (2)(3)

She will find US THERE....Elle **nous y** trouvera
         (1) (4)   (1) (4)

THERE ARE two OF THEM...Il **y en** a deux
    (4)   (5)   (4)(5)

I gave IT TO HIM.... Je **le lui** ai donné

    (2)   (3)   (2)(3)

EXCEPTION: Imperative AFFIRMATIVE:

- Pronouns attached with a hyphen
- Pronouns take the same order as the English (usually)

> Donnez-LE-MOI ! = Give it (to) me !   Note: −(2)−(1)
> Envoyez-LES-LUI! = Send them to him !

Imperative Negative normal: Ne **ME LE** donnez pas !
                           Ne **LES LUI** envoyez pas !

§12. DISJUNCTIVE PRONOUNS (Emphatic or stressed pronouns)

1. Meaning:

moi	= me	*corresponds to* je	)	
toi	= you	” tu	)	
lui	= him	” il	)	
elle	= her	” elle	)	**SUBJECT PRONOUNS**
soi	= 'one'	” on	)	
nous	= us	” nous	)	
vous	= you	” vous	)	
eux	= them (m)	” ils	)	
elles	= them (f)	” elles	)	

2. Usage:

(a) with prepositions

devant moi = in front of me	chez eux = at their home
avec elles = with them	entre nous = between us
pour toi = for you	en face de lui = opposite him

(b) with c'est and ce sont:

c'est moi	= it's me	c'est nous	= It's us
c'est toi	= it's you	c'est vous	= It's you
c'est lui	= It's him	**but** ce *sont* eux	= It's them (masc)
c'est elle	= It's her	ce *sont* elles	= It's them (fem)

(c) for emphasis:

−**Lui**, il est bête! = *He* is stupid !
−**Moi**, j'ai raison! = *I* am right !

(d) in comparisons:

−Il est plus grand que **MOI**   = He is taller than me.

(e) Alone:

— Qui a parlé ? — **Lui** ! = Who spoke? — Him !

(f) Combined with même*(=self) : (for further strengthening)

— Je l'ai fait moi-**même** = I did it mySELF
— Nous l'avons fait nous-**mêmes** = We did it ourSELVES

(g) Double subjects:

— Jean et **moi**, (nous) sommes allés au cinéma. (Not *je*—)
— LUI et elle sont en retard. (Not *il*)

(h) To indicate possession:

— Ce livre est à **moi** = This book is mine.
— Cette usine est **à nous** = That factory is ours.

(i) Idiomatic uses of SOI:

Chacun pour **soi** = Every man for himself.
On travaille pour **soi** = One works for oneself. (literally)

*Note: Other meanings of même.

(i) *even:* Aimez *même* vos ennemis! = Love *even* your enemies!
(ii) *same:* Ils sont du *même* âge = They are the *same* age.
En *même* temps = At the *same* time.

§13. INTERROGATIVE PRONOUNS

1. Subject and object

	PERSON	THING
SUBJECT	**QUI ? = WHO ?** (Qui est-ce qui ?) Qui parle ? Qui est-ce qui parle ? = Who speaks ?	**QU'EST-CE QUI = WHAT ?** (No short form) Qu'est-ce qui vous surprend ? = What surprises you ?
OBJECT	**QUI ? = WHOM ?** (Qui est-ce que ?) Qui cherches-tu ? Qui est-ce que tu cherches ? = Whom are you looking for?	**QUE ? = WHAT ?** (Qu'est-ce que ?) Que pensez-vous ? Qu'est-ce que vous pensez ? = What do you think ?
Note: THERE IS NO INVERSION AFTER THE LONG FORMS		

Note these examples:

Qu'est-ce que c'est ?	= What is it ?
Qu'est-ce que c'est que ça(cela)	= What is that ?
Que faire ?	= What can be done ? (What can I, he, etc... do ?)
Qu'y a-t-il ? Qu'est-ce qu'il y a ?	= What's the matter ?
Qu'est-il devenu ?	= What has become of him ?

2. **à qui ?** = **Whose...?** (*Dont* can never introduce a question)

À qui est la bicyclette ? = Whose is the bicycle ?

3. **Quoi ?** = **what, (stressed form)**

(a) used alone:

QUOI ? Qu'est-ce qu'il a dit ?   ⎫
= WHAT ? What did he say ?   ⎬ Interrogative
                                              ⎭

QUOI ! C'est toi !   ⎫
= WHAT ! It's you !   ⎬ Exclamation
                             ⎭

(b) used with de

QUOI de nouveau ? = What news ? What's new ?

(c) After prepositions:

De quoi parle-t-il ? = What is he talking about ?
À quoi pensez-vous ? = What are you thinking about ?

4. **Lequel ?** = **Which (one) ?**

	MASC	FEM	
SING	lequel ?	laquelle ?	— Refer to a previous noun
PLUR	lesquels ?	lesquelles ?	— Agree in gender and number with it.

— Refer to a previous noun
— Agree in gender and number with it.
— Stand on their own.

Voici deux pommes; **laquelle** voulez-vous ?
= Here are two apples; which (one) do you want ?
J'ai évité un de ses frères. — **Lequel ?**
= I have avoided one of his brothers - Which (one) ?

§14. INTERROGATIVE ADJECTIVES
— QUEL ? = WHICH/WHAT + NOUN

	MASC	FEM	
SING	quel__?	quelle__?	— Stand with a noun.
PLUR	quels__?	quelles__?	— Agree in gender and number with it.

Quelle pomme veux-tu ?   Quelle heure est-il ?
Quel jour sommes-nous ?   Quelles voitures ? Quels stylos ?

Note these exclamations:

Quelle jolie robe !   = What a pretty dress ! (Note the omission *of the*
                                                      article in the French)

Quel dommage !   = What a pity !

Que je suis fatigué !   = How tired I am !
Comme il est content !   = How happy he is !
Comment ! Tu ne l'as pas fait ! = What ! You haven't done it !

§15. DEMONSTRATIVE ADJECTIVES

1. Forms

	MASC	FEM
SING	ce (**cet** before a vowel/mute *h*)	cette
PLUR	ces	ces

2. Meanings

(a) **this/that** (singular)
ce stylo = this/that pen
cet arbre = this/that tree
cet homme = this/that man
cette poche = this/that pocket

(b) **these/those** (plural)
ces tables = these/those tables

3. Meanings stressed.

To emphasize the difference between $\begin{cases} \text{this/that} \\ \text{these/those} \end{cases}$ add $\begin{cases} -\textbf{ci} \\ -\textbf{là} \end{cases}$ to the noun)

     (a) − **ci**:   J'aime ce livre-ci = I like this book
                  J'aime ces pommes-ci = I like these apples

     (b) −**là**:   J'aime cette cravate-là = I like that tie
                  J'aime ces livres-là = I like those books

Note the rule of thumb:
    This (here) book ! .....   − **ci**   (remember, ici = here)
    That (there) book ! ...   − **là**   (remember, là = there)

    Ce livre-ci est rouge, mais cette balle-là est bleue
    = **This** book is red, but **that** ball is blue

§16. DEMONSTRATIVE PRONOUNS

1. Forms:

	MASC	FEM
SING	celui	celle
PLUR	ceux	celles

2. Usage and Meanings:

The Demonstrative Pronoun is always linked to one of the following (a)**de**, (b) **-ci or -là**, (c) **Relative Pronoun**(Sec. 19) the various meanings are given in the examples below.

(a) **Celui de = the ones of, those of , (Paul)'s**
    Celui de Paul est noir = Paul's (= the one of Paul) is black.
    Les chemises de Jean sont jaunes, mais **celles de** Paul sont bleues.
    = John's shirts are yellow, but Paul's are blue.

(b) **Celui-ci, celui-là** = this one, that one
    Celui-ci est rouge, mais **celle-là** est noire.
    = This one is red, but that one (fem) is black.
    Ceux-ci sont jolis, et **celles-là** sont belles
    = These are pretty, and those (fem) are beautiful.

(c) **Celui qui = the one who (which)**
    Quel élève ? - **Celui qui** attend = Which pupil ? — The one who waits.

    Celui que = the one whom (which)
    Ceux qu'il a tués = The ones whom he killed

    Celui dont = the one (of) whom, which
    Celle dont j'ai besoin = The one (of) which I (have) need.

Note....... CELUI-CI = the latter
CELUI-LÀ = the former

Voilà **une poire** et *un citron*; **celle-là** est verte, *celui-ci* est jaune.
└─────────┘ └────────────┘ *the latter* ─────────┘
└─**the former**─────┘

Rule of Thumb: Note that the (CELUI)-LÀ refers to the noun which is
FARTHER AWAY

3. Neuter Demonstrative Pronouns.... Ceci = this
Cela = that (ça in conversation)
These pronouns DO NOT refer to specific nouns.
They refer to general statements of facts, proposals, ideas.
They DO NOT agree in gender and numbers.
CECI est incroyable   = **This** is incredible (some event, etc.)
Que pensez-vous de **CELA** = What do you think of **that** (idea)
Ça m'intéresse   = **That** interests me (a proposal)

4. IT IS – C'EST and IL EST

(a)   C'est + noun or pronoun
C'est mon père   C'était Marie.   C'est lui = It's him
C'est un avion = It is a plane   Ce *sont* eux/elles = It's them
Ce *sont* des avions = They are planes   (See Section 12)

(b) C'est + adjective + full stop
C'est difficile. C'est vrai. C'est impossible.

(c) Il est + adjective + de + infinitive
que + clause

Il est difficile *de comprendre.*   Il est vrai *qu'il est paresseux.*
It is difficult to understand .   It is true that he is lazy.

(d)   Il est/ils sont
Elle est/elles sont + adjective + full stop; *referring to a specific noun.*
....le stylo ?   – **Il est** bleu. = It is blue
....les cahiers ? – **Ils sont** bleus.= They are blue
....cette robe ? – **Elle est** jolie.= It is pretty
....ces fleurs ? – **Elles sont** jolies.= They are pretty

Note 1: **Il est** *and* **elle est** *with professions, nationality, religion.*
Il est __ dentiste.   Elle est __ Américaine. (article omitted)
But: C'est *un* dentiste. C'est *une* Américaine. (See section 26)

Note 2: **Il est** *for time expressions.*
Il est six heures.

Note 3: *Any tense may be used with* **ce:**

E.g: *Future:* ce *sera* utile = It will be useful
Imperfect: C'*étaient* eux = It was them (state/description)
Perfect: ç' a *été* assez = It was enough (event)
(Note the ç before the vowel; see Sections 20 and 35)

§17. POSSESSIVE ADJECTIVES

	M.S.	F.S.	M&F.P.
my	mon	ma	mes
your	ton	ta	tes
his/her	son	sa	ses
its/one's			
our	notre	notre	nos
your	votre	votre	vos
their	leur	leur	leurs

Adjectives **Stand with** the **Noun**
They agree in **gender** and **number**
with the noun they accompany,
NOT with the possessor.

Où est **MON** stylo ?

Where is **MY** pen ?

Il a volé **MA** règle
He has stolen **my** ruler

Jean a cassé **nos** assiettes
Jean has broken **our** plates.

Note 1. The adjective agrees with
the noun. . . .

SON frère = $\left\{ \begin{array}{l} \text{his brother} \\ \text{her brother} \end{array} \right.$

SA soeur = $\left\{ \begin{array}{l} \text{his sister} \\ \text{her sister} \end{array} \right.$

Note 2: MA TA SA not to be used
before a vowel or 'h' mute.
   son arrivée = HIS/HER arrival(F.S.)
   mon auto = MY car (F.S.)
   ton histoire = your story (F.S.)

Note 3: Emphasize the possession by
   (a) *à + disjunctive*
C'est son problème **à lui** !
= That's **his** problem !

   (b) *propre = own*
Il a sa **propre** bicyclette
= He has **his own** bicycle.

Note 4:
   Il est de mes amis $\left. \begin{array}{l} \\ \\ \end{array} \right\}$ = He is
   C'est un de mes amis $\left. \begin{array}{l} \\ \\ \end{array} \right\}$ one of
                                    my friends.

§18. POSSESSIVE PRONOUNS

	M.S.	F.S.
mine	le mien	la mienne
yours	le tien	la tienne
his/hers	le sien	la sienne
ours	le nôtre	la nôtre
yours	le vôtre	la vôtre
their	le leur	la leur
	M.P.	**F.P.**
mine	les miens	les miennes
yours	les tiens	les tiennes
his/hers	les siens	les siennes
ours	les nôtres	les nôtres
yours	les vôtres	les vôtres
theirs	les leurs	les leurs

Pronouns take the place of NOUNS
They stand ALONE.
They agree in gender and number with the
noun replaced, NOT with the possessor.

J'ai mon stylo et ma soeur a **LE SIEN***
I have my pen and my sister has **HERS**

Sa maison est près de **LA MIENNE**
His/her house is near **mine.**

Va chercher des assiettes — Jean a cassé
les nôtres
Fetch some plates — Jean has broken **ours.**

Note 1 *: The pronoun agrees with
the replaced noun . . . .

$\left. \begin{array}{l} \text{le sien} \\ \text{les siennes} \\ \text{la sienne} \end{array} \right\}$ = $\left\{ \begin{array}{l} \text{his} \\ \text{hers} \end{array} \right.$

LA montre: Il a **LA SIENNE** (=his)
LE livre: Elle a **LE SIEN** (=hers)

Note 2: à and de combine with le and les.
   example:
   Mon livre est près **DU** sien
   My book is near HIS

Note 3: MINE, etc., after être: à +
disjunctive pronoun.
Ce livre est **à moi** = . . **mine**
Ce cahier est **à lui** = . . **his**

§19. RELATIVE PRONOUNS

A, QUI QUE (QU') DONT

These pronouns refer to a previously mentioned **NOUN**

1. Subject – Qui = who, which, that.
   (a) **Who:** L'homme **qui**→est grand = The man **who** is tall.
   (b) **Which, that:** Les trains **QUI**→ sont bleus = The trains {**which** **(that** are blue

2. Object – Que (Qu')= whom, which, that.

   (a) **Whom:** L'homme **que** vous avez vu = The man **whom** you have seen.

   (b) **Which, that:** Le train **qu'il a** manqué = The train {**(which** **(that** he missed.

NOTE THE 'RULE OF THUMB'
   (i) *QUI goes next to the verb* . . . . .QUI→est.. . . . .
(not counting 'ne' and object pronouns, e.g:
L'élève QUI n' EST pas sage = The pupil who is not well-behaved.
L'homme QUI l' A tué = The man who killed him)

   (ii) *Que (qu') does not go next to the verb:* . . . . que J' ai . . . .

3. Possessive – **Dont** = whose, of whom, of which (really = **DE + QUE/QU'**)
   (a) **Whose:** La dame **dont** le mari est riche.
     = The lady **whose** husband is rich.
   (b) **Of whom:** L'homme **dont** j'ai entendu parler.
     = The man **(of) whom** I've heard.
   (c) **Of which:** L'argent **dont** vous avez besoin.
     = The money **of which** you have need.
           (= which you need)

Note 1. 'Rule of Thumb' - Dont really means de + que
   (a) La dame **que** le mari **de** est riche   = **DONT**
   (b) L'homme **que** j'ai entendu parler **de**   = **DONT**
   (c) L'argent **que** j'ai besoin **de**   = **DONT**

Note 2. The Relative Pronoun is never omitted in French.
   Le livre **dont** j'ai besoin = The book (which) I need.
   Le garçon **que** j'ai vu = The boy (whom) I saw.
   La pomme **que** j'ai voléE = The apple (which) I stole

Note 3. Expressions
   . . . .la façon DONT . . . = ...the way in which . . .
   le mot DONT je me souviens (se souvenir DE)
   l'argent DONT j'ai besoin (avoir besoin DE)

Note 4: DONT can never introduce a question . . . .use 'À QUI ' :
   À QUI sont les assiettes ? = Whose are the plates ?

B. CE QUI CE QUE (CE QU') CE DONT

   - These pronouns refer to a previous **idea**, not a specific noun,
    unlike   Qui, Que (Qu'), Dont.
   - They also introduce Indirect Questions.

   1. Subject – CE QUI = what, which, **when summing up a sentence or IDEA**
   (a) **What** (idea): Je me demandais **ce qui** était arrivé = I wondered
               what had happened.

(b) which (idea): Ils disent qu'ils vont partir, **ce qui** est vrai
= They say that they are going to go, **which** is true

2. **Object – Ce Que (Ce Qu')** = What.

NO SPECIFIC NOUN	Je lui ai demandé **ce qu'**il avait fait. = I asked him **what** he had done. **Ce que** je préfère, c'est qu'il ne parle plus. = **what** I prefer is that he doesn't speak any longer.

3. **Possessive – ce dont** = of what, about what (really = DE + CE QUE).
Savez-vous **ce dont** il parle ? = Do you know **what** he is talking **about** ?
(obviously CE QUE + DE, since the verb is parler DE, see above)

ce dont vous parlez ne m'intéresse pas = **what** you're talking **about** doesn't
interest me.

(Again, obviously, CE QUE + DONT. Study/contrast examples of *dont*
on facing page).

C. RELATIVE PRONOUNS AFTER PREPOSITIONS

1. FOR THINGS:

	MASCULINE	FEMININE
SINGULAR	Lequel	Laquelle
PLURAL	Lesquels	Lesquelles

with which: Voici le fusil AVEC LEQUEL j'ai tué le soldat.   (M.S.)
on which: La chaise SUR LAQUELLE vous êtes assis.   (F.S.)
amongst which: Les feuilles PARMI LESQUELLES j'ai vu un oiseau. (F.P.)

Note 1:   à and **de** combine with lequel, lesquelles etc., as follows:

	MASCULINE	FEMININE	MASCULINE	FEMININE
SINGULAR	auquel	à laquelle	duquel	de laquelle
PLURAL	auxquels	auxquelles	desquels	desquelles

in the middle of which: Le parc AU MILIEU DUQUEL il y a un lac
to which: Le parc AUQUEL il est allé.
in whose: La victime DANS la chambre DE LAQUELLE (or *de qui* *)
on a trouvé la lettre.
(* or *de qui* when relating to a person)

Note 2:   in/on which often means *where*
La chaise **où** vous êtes assis = The chair ON WHICH (=where) you
are sitting.
(*Remember:* **Là où** = where at the start of a sentence)

2. **FOR PEOPLE:**   QUI may be used to mean **whom** after prepositions:
à QUI = to whom....Mes amis, **à qui** je parlais . . .
de QUI = of whom....Ses amis, **de qui** tu parlais . . .
avec QUI = with whom....Jean, **avec qui** j'ai quitté la . . .

3. **IDIOMATIC NEUTER FORM:** QUOI = which, what; not referring to a specific noun.
E.g: Après **quoi**, il est parti = After WHICH, he left.
Dis-moi de **quoi** tu as besoin = Tell me WHAT you need.
(not *dont* because no specific noun is mentioned)
Sur **quoi**, il est parti =   (Whereupon) he left.
(Upon which)

§20. ACCENTS

1. (é) **Acute = AIGU**: used over an *e*
   l'été, énorme, j'ai pénétré

2. (è) **Grave = GRAVE**: used over (*a:* à, là
                                    (*e:* la mère
                                    (*u:* où
   Some verbs take a grave accent before a mute (unsounded) ending:
   j'achète, tu mènes, il lève, ils espèrent. (See page 5)

3. (ê) **Circumflex = CIRCONLEXE**: when used over *a, e, i, o, u,* the sound
                                              is lengthened.

un âne	=	donkey (aSS)	un hôte	=	hoSt
la bête	=	beaSt	le.coût	=	coSt
une île	=	iSland			

   Note that the (∧) often indicates the absence of an s
   This is also indicated by a (´) in certain words:
         un école = **S**chool
         une éponge = **S**ponge

4. (ë) **Diaeresis = TRÉMA**: used over *e, i, u;* indicates separate pronunciation
                                      of preceding vowel.

Noël	=	Christmas
naïf (f. naïve)	=	naïve
Saül	=	Saul

5. (ç) **Cedilla = CÉDILLE**: used to 'soften' c before *a, o, u*. (produces s sound)

	SOFT *(with ş)*	HARD *(no ş)*
a	la façade	le cadeau
o	la leçon	confident
u	le reçu	reculer

Examples of (ç) in –cer verbs: *

Present Participle:	commenÇant	(before *a*)
Imperfect:	je commenÇais	(*a*)
Past Historic:	il commenÇa	(*a*)
Present:	nous commenÇons	(*o*)
Past Participle:	j'ai aperÇu	(*u*)

Note also: g may be 'cushioned' by adding **e** before *a* and *o*
Examples of this added E in –ger verbs: *

Present Participle:	mangEant	(before *a*)
Imperfect:	je mangEais	(*a*)
Past Historic:	il mangEa	(*a*)
Present:	nous mangEons	(*o*)

(* See pages 4 and 10 for more examples)

§21. ADJECTIVES

A. FEMININE FORMS

1. Add an *e* to the masculine

court ⟶ courtE	= short	
noir ⟶ noirE	= black	
méchant ⟶ méchantE	= wicked (naughty, of children)	

2. Those already ending in an *e* remain unchanged

jeune ⟶ jeune	= young
rouge ⟶ rouge	= red

3. Basic Patterns

(a)	-er ⟶ -ère	:	fier ⟶ fière	=	proud
(b)	-eux ⟶ -euse	:	soigneux ⟶ soigneuse	=	careful
(c)	-f ⟶ -ve	:	oisif ⟶ oisive	=	idle
(d)	-en ⟶ -enne	:	ancien ⟶ ancienne	=	former
(e)	-el ⟶ -elle	:	solennel ⟶ solennelle	=	solemn
(f)	-et ⟶ -ette	:	muet ⟶ muette	=	dumb/mute

4. Common Irregularities.

beau ⟶ belle	= beautiful	frais ⟶ fraîche	=	fresh
nouveau ⟶ nouvelle	= new	public ⟶ publique	=	public
vieux ⟶ vieille	= old	favori ⟶ favorite	=	favourite
fou ⟶ folle	= mad	gentil ⟶ gentille	=	nice/kind
bon ⟶ bonne	= good	gros ⟶ grosse	=	large/fat
long ⟶ longue	= long	bas ⟶ basse	=	low
blanc ⟶ blanche	= white	épais ⟶ épaisse	=	thick
doux ⟶ douce	= sweet/soft	faux ⟶ fausse	=	false
sec ⟶ sèche	= dry	aigu ⟶ aiguë	=	sharp
malin ⟶ maligne	= sly, evil minded.			
		roux ⟶ rousse	=	red (of hair)
grec ⟶ grecque	= Greek	mou ⟶ molle	=	soft
sot ⟶ sotte	= silly, foolish	gras ⟶ grasse	=	fat (of meat)

B. PLURAL FORMS

1. Add an *s* to the masculine or feminine singular

court ⟶ courts	
noirE ⟶ noirEs	
méchant ⟶ méchants	

2. Masculine Singular ending in -*x*, -*s*, are unchanged.

Masc. Sing	Masc. Plur	FEMININE
heureux ⟶ heureux		heureuse ⟶ heureuses
gros ⟶ gros		grosse ⟶ grosses
	UNCHANGED	

3. Masculine Singular ending in -EAU and -EU : ADD x

				FEMININE
(a) -EAU :	beau ⟶ beaux	= beautiful	belle ⟶ belles
	nouveau ⟶ nouveaux	= new	nouvelle ⟶ nouvelles
(b) -EU* :	hébreu ⟶ hébreux	= Hebrew	hébraïque ⟶ hébraïques
(exception	bleu ⟶ bleus	= blue	bleue ⟶ bleues)
(* Rare)			

4. Masculine Singular ending in -AL : CHANGE TO aux

		FEMININE
amical ⟶ amicaux	= friendly	amicale ⟶ amicales
général ⟶ généraux	= general	générale ⟶ générales
égal ⟶ égaux	= equal	égale ⟶ égales

C. SPECIAL MASCULINE SINGULAR FORM before a vowel or mute *h*

beau ⟶	le **bel** acteur	= the handsome actor
nouveau ⟶	le **nouvel** élève	= the new pupil
vieux ⟶	le **vieil** hôtel	= the old hotel
fou ⟶	le **fol** * espoir	= the mad hope
mou ⟶	le **mol** * édredon	= the soft eiderdown (* Rare)

D. POSITION OF ADJECTIVES

1. Before the Noun

The following adjectives normally stand **BEFORE** the noun
(All other adjectives normally go after the noun)

joli	=	pretty	grand	=	large	méchant	=	naughty
vieux	=	old	beau	=	beautiful	excellent	=	excellent
jeune	=	young	gros	=	big	vilain	=	ugly
petit	=	small	large	=	wide	tout	=	all
court	=	short	meilleur	=	better	tel	=	such
gentil	=	nice,kind	haut	=	high	autre	=	other
long	=	long	mauvais	=	bad	*(and all numbers)*		

2. Two adjectives

(a) **Both from the list** (above) - place both **before**
une **jolie petite** maison   =   a pretty little house

(b) **Only one from the list** - place it **before,** the other *after*
une **grande** tasse *rouge*   =   a large red cup
de **petits** cahiers *bleus*   =   (some) small blue exercise books

(c) **Neither from the list** - place both *after, linked with et*
une chambre *froide et sombre* = a cold and dark bedroom

E. CHANGED MEANING BY CHANGED POSITION

		BEFORE	AFTER
PROPRE (propre)	*(Own* *(Clean*	**OWN** ses propres dents = his OWN teeth	**CLEAN** des chemises propres = (some) CLEAN shirts
ANCIEN (ancienne)	*(Former* *(Ancient*	**FORMER** un ancien soldat = a FORMER soldier	**ANCIENT** une église ancienne = an ANCIENT church
DERNIER (dernière)	*(The Last* *(Last*	**THE LAST(in a series)** la dernière semaine de mes vacances = THE LAST week of my holidays	**LAST (just gone)** la semaine dernière, je suis allé au cinéma = LAST week, I went to the cinema
PROCHAIN (prochaine)	*(The Next* *(Next*	**THE NEXT (in a series)** la prochaine fois = THE NEXT TIME but: la semaine suivante	**NEXT (Immediate future)** la semaine prochaine,.. = NEXT week
PAUVRE (pauvre)	*(Pitiable* *(Penniless*	**PITIABLE** Oh ! mon pauvre ami ! Oh ! my POOR friend !	**PENNILESS** une femme pauvre = a PENNILESS/POOR woman
GRAND (grande)	*(Great* *(Tall*	**GREAT** un grand soldat = a GREAT soldier	**TALL** un soldat grand = a TALL soldier
CHER (chère)	*(Dear* *(Expensive*	**DEAR** mon cher oncle = my DEAR uncle	**EXPENSIVE** une montre chère = an EXPENSIVE/DEAR watch

§22. ADVERBS

A. FORMATION: Basic rule, add **- MENT** *(= -LY)* to the feminine form of
the adjective.

1. FEMININE ADJECTIVES

MASCULINE		FEMININE		ADVERB		MEANING
heureux	⟶	heureuse	⟶	heureusement	=	happily
rapide	⟶	rapide	⟶	rapidement	=	rapidly
premier	⟶	première	⟶	premièrement	=	firstly

2. MASCULINE ADJECTIVES ending in a vowel

- **MENT** is added directly to masculine adjectives ending in a vowel

MASCULINE	ADVERB	MEANING
poli ⟶	poli**ment**	= politely
vrai ⟶	vrai**ment**	= truly
(*EXCEPTION* gai ⟶	gaie**ment**	= gaily)

3. ADJECTIVES ending in ' -ANT' or ' -ENT'

Adjectives ending in ' -ANT' or ' -ENT' change the ' -NT' to 'M'

élégant ⟶	élég**amment**	= elegantly
violent ⟶	viol**emment**	= violently
évident ⟶	évid**emment**	= evidently
(*Exception:* lent ⟶	lente**ment**	= slowly)

4. IRREGULAR ADVERBS

ADJECTIVE		ADVERB		
bon	=	good ⟶	**bien**	= well
mauvais	=	bad ⟶	**mal**	= badly
meilleur	=	better ⟶	**mieux**	= better
petit	=	small ⟶	**peu**	= little
gentil	=	kind ⟶	**gentiment**	= kindly
précis	=	precise ⟶	**précisément**	= precisely
énorme	=	enormous ⟶	**énormément**	= enormously
profond	=	deep ⟶	**profondément**	= deeply
aveugle	=	blind ⟶	**aveuglément**	= blindly

B. POSITION OF ADVERBS *NEVER* * between *VERB & SUBJECT* in French

SUBJECT	ADVERB	VERB	
I	**often**	smile	= Je* souris **souvent**
The window	**suddenly**	opened	= **Soudain,** la fenêtre* s'est ouverte
They	**quickly**	carried	= Ils* ont **vite** porté

§23. AGAIN

1. 're' + VERB

Je dois **re**lire le livre
= I must read the book AGAIN

Je viens de le **re**faire
= I have just done it AGAIN

2. DE NOUVEAU = anew

Je l'ai fait **de nouveau**
= I did it AGAIN

3. ENCORE (une fois) = (once) again

Il l'a fait **encore une fois**
= He did it (once) AGAIN

§24. ALL and EVERY

1. TOUT LE + NOUN   (= all the ....) Note agreements of the following:

M.S.	Tout le gâteau = all the cake
F.S.	Toute la journée = all day (long)
M.P.	Tous les jours = every day . . . . . . (see 2 (a) below)
F.P.	Toutes les fois que.. = every time that . . .. . . (see 2 (b) below)

(Note: Tous les deux sont en retard = *Both* are late)
Tout le monde est heureux = Everybody is happy (Singular Verb)

2. CHAQUE + NOUN = EACH/EVERY	**2. CHACUN/CHACUNE = EACH ONE**
Chaque *is an adjective and stands with a NOUN*	**Chacun/Chacune** *are pronouns and replace the NOUN*
(a) Il le fait chaque jour = He does it each/every day	(a) CHACUNE est très jolie (F.S.) EACH (one) is very pretty
(b) Chaque fois qu'il mange = each/every time that he eats	(b) CHACUN de ces faits .....(M.S.) EACH (one) of these facts......

3. TOUS and TOUTES = ALL, (i.e.everybody) M.P. & F.P.
      (a) Ils sont **tous** contents = They are ALL happy
      (b) Elles sont **toutes** revenues = They have ALL returned

4. TOUT = ALL (i.e. everything)   Neuter and invariable (i.e. does not agree)

    (a) **Tout** dépend de moi =   (everything) depends on me.
                              (ALL   )
    (b) J'ai **tout** perdu   =   I have lost   (everything
                                    (ALL

5. TOUT as an ADVERB = all, quite, altogether, very

Adverbs do NOT normally agree, but, to preserve the feminine SOUND,
TOUT ' agrees ' in front of a **FEMININE ADJECTIVE** beginning with a **CONSONANT**

'AGREEMENT'		**'NON - AGREEMENT'**
Toute fatigué E	(F.S.)	tout* épuisée (F.S.) tout seul (M.S.)
Toutes fatigué ES	(F.P.)	tout* épuisées (F.P.) tout seuls (M.P.)
		* Liaison provides the feminine sound

Examples: Elle était **toute** fatiguée = she was quite tired (F.S.)
                Elle était tout* épuisée = she was quite exhausted   (F.S.)
                Elles étaient **toutes** seules = They were quite alone (F.P.)

§25. ALLER + INFINITIVE

1. Immediate Future tense: (See Page 7)

Je vais nager   = I *am going* to swim

2. Imperfect continuous: (See Page 50)

Elle allait mourir = She *was going* to die

§26. ARTICLES

A. TYPES

1. Definite Article	le, la, l', les	= the
2. Indefinite Article	un, une, (des)	= a, an (some)
3. Partitive Article	*du, de la, de l', des, de, d'*	*= some,_____, any (See Section 48)*

THE Singular	*masculine* LE *feminine* LA	} L'	before a vowel or mute 'h'	A (AN) Singular	*masculine* UN *feminine* UNE
THE Plural	*masculine and feminine*	} LES		SOME Plural	*masculine and feminine* } DES

B. NOTES ON THE INDEFINITE ARTICLE

1. When used in French, but not in English

- with an abstract noun qualified by an adjective.

avec **une** simplicité totale = with _____ total simplicity

2. When omitted in French but used in English

(a) With job, nationality, religion

Il est __ professeur,   il est __ français,   il est __catholique
(or, c'est un professeur)

He is **A** teacher,   he is **A** Frenchman,   he is **A** catholic.

(b) In apposition

Manchester, __ ville de plaisir, est très agréable.

Manchester, **A** city of pleasure, is very agreeable.

(c) After Quel . . . . . . '   (See Section 14, Interrogative Adjectives)

Quelle __ jolie robe ! = What **A** pretty dress !

C. NOTES ON THE DEFINITE ARTICLE

1. When used in French but not in English
(a) Before many nouns

La nuit tombait = __ Night was falling
Je cherche **le** bonheur = I look for____ happiness.

(b) With parts of the body (instead of mon, ma, mes, etc)

Il ferme **les** yeux = he closes his eyes

NOTE 1.   Action to one's person : use *Reflexive Pronoun*
              Je *me* brosse les cheveux = I brush *my* hair

NOTE 2.   Action to another person : use *lui or leur*
              Je *lui* brosse les cheveux = I brush *his/her* hair

(c) Formal address, titles, rank, before certain adjectives

Monsieur **LE** facteur = (Mr)__ Postman . . . .
LE roi Louis XIV = __ King Louis XIV
Monsieur **LE** capitaine = __Captain . . . .
LE pauvre Claude = __ Poor Claude

(d) Names of Countries

    J'ai visité **LA** France = I have visited __France

2. When omitted in French

in long lists:

Tous étaient blessés —__soldats,__policiers,__pompiers,__brancardiers.
= All were wounded — soldiers, policemen, firemen, stretcherbearers.

3. SINGULAR IN FRENCH, PLURAL IN ENGLISH

LA flamme des bougies = the flames of the candles (each candle has **ONE** flame)
Les hommes ont mis **leur veston** = The men put on their jackets
                              (each man has **ONE** jacket)

§ 27. AVOIR EXPRESSIONS

avoir froid	= to be cold		avoir faim	= to be hungry
avoir chaud	= to be hot		avoir soif	= to be thirsty
avoir tort	= to be wrong		avoir peur	= to be afraid
avoir raison	= to be right		avoir honte =	to be ashamed

avoir l'air   = to seem
avoir sommeil   = to be sleepy
avoir mal **à**   = to have something wrong with (pain in)
avoir besoin **DE** = to need
avoir dix ans   = to be 10 years old
avoir envie **DE** = to be inclined to, to feel like (+Infinitive)

EXAMPLES

J'ai besoin **DE** dix francs	= I need 10 francs	Il a raison	= he is right
J'avais mal aux dents	= I had toothache	J'ai chaud	= I am hot
J'ai mal **à** la tête	= I have a headache	Elle a l'air triste = She seems sad	
J'ai seize ans	= I am 16 years old		
Nous avons sommeil	= we are sleepy		
J'ai envie **DE** manger	= I feel like eating		

NOTE 1:   *ÊTRE + adjective is used for the temperature of food or drinks*
       Mon café *est* froid   =   my coffee is cold
       La soupe *est* chaude =   the soup is hot

NOTE 2:   *FAIRE + adjective is used for weather*
       Il *FAIT* froid   =   It is cold (See Section 71)

§28. CHEZ

1. AT/TO the house (home) of

chez moi = at (to) my house (home)

chez toi = at/to your house (home)	chez nous = at/to our house (home)
chez lui = at/to his house (home)	chez vous = at/to your house(home)
chez elle = at/to her house (home)	chez eux = at/to their(m) house(home)
chez soi = at/to one's house(home)	chez elles = at/to their(f) house(home)

e.g.   Ils rentrent chez **EUX** = They go home.
      Je viendrai chez **TOI** = I shall come to your house.
      On rentre chez **SOI** = One (literally) goes home.

NOTE: *à la maison*   can still be used
      Je vais chez mon oncle
      Je vais à la maison de mon oncle

2. CHEZ for the DOCTOR'S and DENTIST'S

Je vais chez le médecin = I am going to the doctor's
Il est allé chez le dentiste = He has gone to the dentist's

3. CHEZ and the SHOPKEEPER

Je vais chez le boulanger = I go to the baker's
Je vais à la boulangerie = I go to the bakery

	MAN	WOMAN	THE SHOP
baker	le boulanger	la boulangère	la boulangerie
pastry-cook	le pâtissier	la pâtissière	la pâtisserie
butcher	le boucher	la bouchère	la boucherie
grocer	l'épicier	l'épicière	l'épicerie
	USE CHEZ	**USE CHEZ**	**USE à la**

§29. COLOURS

white	= blanc/blanche	yellow	= jaune
black	= noir(e)	pink	= rose
blue	= bleu(e)	grey	= gris(e)
green	= vert(e)	orange	= orange *
red	= rouge	purple	= pourpre
red(hair)	= roux/rousse	brown	= brun(e)
blond,fair	= blond(e)	brown	= marron *

light blue	= bleu **clair** *	** NEVER AGREE*
dark blue	= bleu **foncé** *	des yeux *bleu clair* des rideaux *orange*
blui**sh**	= bleu**âtre**	une robe *bleu foncé* des souliers *marron*

§30. COMBINATIONS: À, DE

1. AT THE / TO THE / IN THE

MS	à + le =	**au**	Je donne le livre **au** garçon (=to the)
FS	à + la =	à la	Je suis à la bibliothèque (=at the)
M & FS	à + l' =	à l' *	Je le donne à l'élève (= to the)
M & FP	à + les =	**aux**	Je suis **aux** champs (=in the)

* Before a vowel or mute 'h'

2. (a) FROM THE; OF THE, indicating possession.
   (b) SOME, ANY (PARTITIVE, see Section 48)

MS	de + le =	**du**	Le livre **du** garçon (= of the)
FS	de + la =	de la	La robe de la jeune fille (= of the)
M & FS	de + l' =	de l' *	Je descends de l'avion (=from the)
M & FP	de + les =	des	Je mange **des** bonbons (=some)

*
Before a vowel or mute 'h'

§31. COMPARATIVE & SUPERLATIVE   1. Adjectives   2. Adverbs

A. COMPARATIVE

1. ADJECTIVES   (taller   )   of **two** persons or things
                (**more** tall)

Jean est **plus** grand **que** Pierre = more tall (=taller) than Peter
Georges est **moins** grand **que** Pierre = less tall than Peter
Hélène est **aussi** grande * **que** Pierre = as tall as Peter
Vous *n'* êtes *pas si* grand **que** Pierre = as tall as (*after a negative*)
(* Adjectives agree as usual)

2. ADVERBS — MORE slowly of **TWO**

Il travaille **plus** lentement **que** Jean   = He works more slowly than John
Il travaille **moins** lentement **que** Jean = He works less slowly than John
Elle travaille **aussi** lentement **que** Marie = She works as slowly as Marie

(Adverbs never agree. However see *tout* Section 24)

B. SUPERLATIVE   add **le, la or les** to the comparative.

1. ADJECTIVES —   (pretti**est**)   of **three** or more persons or things
                (**most** pretty)

(a) Adjectives before the noun

le plus joli chapeau   = the pretti**est** hat
la plus grande maison   = the big**gest** house
les plus grandes valises   = the big**gest** suitcases.

(b) Adjective after the noun

le livre *le plus intéressant*   = the **most** interesting book
le cheval *le plus énorme*   = the **most** enormous horse
les gens *les plus intelligents* = the **most** intelligent people
       (Remember adjectival agreements)

NOTE: In after a superlative is translated by **de**

   e.g.   L'élève le plus paresseux **de** la classe
        = the laziest pupil in the class.

        le meilleur livre **du** monde
        = the best book in the world.

2. ADVERBS – the **most** slowly of **three** or more

> Il court *le plus lentement* = he runs the **most** slowly
> Elle se bat *le plus furieusement* = she fights the **most** furiously

C. IRREGULAR COMPARATIVES and SUPERLATIVES

SIMPLE	COMPARATIVE	SUPERLATIVE
1. ADJECTIVES		
bon = good	meilleur = better	le meilleur = best
mauvais = bad	plus mauvais ⎱ = worse pire ⎰	le plus mauvais ⎱ = the worst le pire ⎰
petit = small	plus petit = smaller	le plus petit = the smallest
	moindre = less (amount or size)	le moindre = the least

SIMPLE	COMPARATIVE	SUPERLATIVE
2. ADVERBS		
bien = well	mieux = better	le mieux = the best
mal = badly	plus mal ⎱ = worse pis * ⎰	le plus mal ⎱ = the worst le pis ⎰
peu = little	moins = less	le moins = the least
beaucoup = much	plus = more	le plus = the most
bientôt = soon	plus tôt = sooner	le plus tôt = the soonest

(* Tant pis ! = So much the worse!   Too bad!)

§32. DATE, DAYS, MONTHS, YEAR, SEASONS

A. DATE: (la date)

le premier mars ←——————The Exception
le deux mars etc ←——————This, and all the rest are normal
le onze mars ←——————Note carefully (not l')
le huit mars ←——————Note carefully (not l')

B. DAYS (les jours)   C. MONTHS (les mois)

lundi	janvier
mardi	février
mercredi	mars
jeudi	avril
vendredi	mai
samedi	juin
dimanche	juillet
	août

> en février ⎱ au mois de février ⎰ in February

septembre
octobre
novembre
décembre

(**NOTE: the small initial letters**)

D. YEAR (L'an)

En mil neuf cent soixante-deux   = in 1962
Le Nouvel An   =   New Year
Le Jour de l'An   =   New Year's Day

E. SEASONS (les saisons)

le printemps .... au printemps   = In Spring
l'été ...... en été   = In Summer
l'automne .... en automne   = In Autumn
l'hiver ..... en hiver   = In Winter

§33. DEVOIR and FALLOIR

A. DEVOIR

Present Tense

Necessity: je dois manger   = (I have to eat
                                        (I must eat

Obligation: je dois travailler   = I (should) work
                                           (ought to)

NOTE: 'supposed to'   'AM TO'
          je dois partir tout à l'heure
          = I **am to** leave presently

Perfect Tense

Necessity: j'ai dû mentir   = (I had to lie
                                        (I have had to lie

Probability: Il a dû partir   =   He must have gone

Past Historic Tense (Simple Past)

Necessity: Je dus mentir   = I had to lie

Imperfect Tense

Necessity:
(Repeated action)

          Je devais me reposer tous les jours
          = I had to (= used to have to) rest every day

Probability - (state)
          Elle devait être heureuse
          = She must have been happy

NOTE: 'supposed to'   'WAS TO'
          je devais arriver à dix heures
          = I **was to** arrive at 10 o' clock

Pluperfect Tense

Necessity   j'avais dû finir = I had had to finish)
(Past Narrative: Il avait dû finir = he must have finished)

Future Tense

Necessity   Je devrai commencer =   I (must   )
                                            (shall have to) begin

Future Perfect Tense

J'aurai dû commencer = I shall have had to begin.

Conditional Tense   = ought to/should

Je devrais partir à six heures
= I (should   )
    (ought to) leave at six o'clock

Conditional Perfect Tense   - ought to HAVE/ should HAVE

J'aurais dû vider la poubelle
= I (should have   )
    (ought to have) emptied the bin.

NOTE 1. DEVOIR also means   to owe, e.g. money

Il me doit dix francs = He owes me ten francs

NOTE 2. avoir à   also can mean   *to have to*

Nous avons à travailler = We have to work

B. FALLOIR   FALLOIR is an impersonal verb (used always in the **il** form)
                      It can be used to imply **necessity** and **need**

1. NECESSITY

Present Tense
Il faut partir .....
= We/One must leave

Perfect Tense
Il a fallu partir .....
= We/one had to leave

Past Historic
Il fallut partir ......
= We/one had to leave

Imperfect Tense
Il fallait oublier ......
= We/one (had to   ) forget
         (used to have to)

Pluperfect Tense
Il avait fallu partir ....
= We/one had had to leave

Future Tense
Il faudra partir ....
= We/one (must   )
         (shall have to)leave

Add an **Indirect Object Pronoun**
to clarify the person and to add emphasis

1. Il **me** faut partir
   = I must leave

2. Il **lui** a fallu partir
   = He had to leave

3. Il **me** fallut partir
   = I had to leave

4. Il **lui** fallait oublier
   = He had to forget

5. Il **m'**avait fallu partir
   = I had had to leave

6. Il **nous** faudra partir
   = We shall have to leave

Future Perfect Tense
Il aura fallu partir ....
= We/one will have had to leave

Conditional Tense
Il faudrait partir ...
= We/one (ought to)
         (should) leave

Conditional Perfect Tense
Il aurait fallu partir ....
We/one (ought to have   ) left
       (should have   )

Indirect Object Pronoun
7. Il **leur** aura fallu partir   = They will have had to leave
8. Il **me** faudrait partir   = I ought to leave
9. Il **lui** aurait fallu partir   He ought to have left

2. NEED (+ NOUN)

e.g.   Il lui faut des livres = He needs some books
       Il me fallait un pistolet = I needed a pistol

compare:

       Il a besoin de livres = He needs some books
       J'avais besoin d'un pistolet = I needed a pistol

NOTE: *ALTERNATIVE TO DEVOIR and FALLOIR for NECESSITY*

       être obligé de   e.g. Je suis obligé d'attendre
                                    = I must/ have to wait

                                    J'ai été obligé de me lever
                                    = I was obliged/ had to get up

§34. DIMENSIONS

A. MEASUREMENTS — use AVOIR or ÊTRE

1. Length

(a) avoir: **Ce camion a 6 mètres de long**
(b) être: Ce camion est long de 6 mètres   (fem. = longue)
                 = This lorry is 6 metres long.

2. Width
(a) avoir: Cette table a 7 mètres de large
(b) être: Cette table est large de 7 mètres
                 = This table is 7 metres wide

3. Height
(a) avoir: Cette échelle a 15 mètres de haut
(b) être: Cette échelle est haute de 15 mètres
                 = This ladder is 15 metres high.

4. Depth
(a) avoir: la mer a 100 mètres de profondeur *
(b) être: la mer est profonde de 100 mètres
              = The sea is 100 metres deep

5. Thickness
(a) avoir: L'arbre a 2 mètres d'épaisseur *
(b) être: L'arbre est épais de 2 mètres (feminine = épaisse)
              = The tree is 2 metres thick

NOTE 1*   *profondeur* and *épaisseur* are nouns, but are used for measurements in the avoir type construction; in all the rest, the adjectives are used as fully exemplified above.

NOTE 2   The French for '*by*' in measurements is as follows:

(a)   **SUR** for avoir type   **(b)**   **ET** for être type

(a)   Cette machine a 3 mètres de long **SUR** 4 mètres de large

(b)   Cette machine est longue de 3 mètres **ET** large de 4 mètres
        = This machine is 3 metres long **BY** 4 metres wide.

B.   **DISTANCE**

Always use **à**
e.g. La bibliothèque est **à** cinq kilomètres **d'ici**

    = The library is five kilomètres **away** (=from here)

§35. ELISION

This is indicated by an apostrophe, when *e, a, or i* are dropped before another vowel.

e.g. l'ami, s'il le pense, puisqu'elle est arrivée, lorsqu'il est parti,
    (*presque* only elides in this case: la presqu'île = peninsula)

NOTE 1:   certain dates; *le* onze avril   *le* huit mai

NOTE 2:   **h** *aspiré* — no elision before certain words beginning with '*h*'.

le hasard	=	chance	**Le** Havre	= place name
la hâte	=	haste	(Hence: **au** Havre = to Le Havre)	
la haie	=	hedge	**du** Havre = from Le Havre)	
le haricot	=	bean		
la haute cuisine	=	high-class cooking		

§36. A FEW . . . . SOME

1. **PEU DE** = *Little*   (i.e., not much)
    J'ai peu de fromage = I have (not much/little) cheese

2. **UN Peu de** = *A little*   (i.e., some)
    J'ai **UN** peu de fromage   = I have (some/a little) cheese

3. **QUELQUE(S)** = *a few/some*   (*NOT* linked by *DE* because it is an adjective)

    (a) *In the plural*

    Il a passé *quelques* jours chez moi
        = He spent a few/some days at my home

    (b) *In the singular*

        J'ai *quelque* vague espoir
        = I have some faint hope

NOTE: **QUELQUE CHOSE DE + ADJECTIVE** = Something. . . .

Quelque chose DE nouveau = something new
Quelque chose D'intéressant = something interesting

4. **QUELQUES-UNS/QUELQUES-UNES** = a few/some

These are pronouns and take the place of nouns. (Contrast quelque(s) which is an adjective and stands with the noun).

    Quelques-uns de mes amis sont riches
    A few/some of my friends are rich

    Quelques-unEs de mes amiEs sont belles
    A few/some of my (female) friends are beautiful

5. **QUELQU'UN** = somebody, someone

Quelqu'un l'a mangé = somebody has eaten it.
J'ai vu **quelqu'un** = I saw somebody.

§37. FOR – PENDANT, POUR, DEPUIS

1. **POUR for FUTURE TIME or INTENDED ACTION**

    Je vais en France **POUR** les grandes vacances
    = I am going to France for the summer holidays

2. **PENDANT for completed PAST time**

    Il est resté à Paris **PENDANT** trois semaines
    = He remained in Paris for three weeks.

3. **DEPUIS for PAST action which is still continuing**   (See Section 69)

    J'attends ici **depuis** dix minutes
    = I have been waiting here for ten minutes

§38. FORMS OF THE VERB

PRESENT	PERFECT
1. AFFIRMATIVE Je * donne Tu * donnes etc.	**1. AFFIRMATIVE** J'*ai donné Tu* as donné etc.
2. NEGATIVE *"Sandwich technique"* Je NE* donne PAS Tu NE* donnes PAS etc.	**2. NEGATIVE** *"Sandwich technique"* Je N'*ai PAS donné Tu N'*as PAS donné etc.
3. INTERROGATIVE *(a) Est-ce que technique* Est-ce que je* donne ? Est-ce que tu* donnes ? *etc.*	**3. INTERROGATIVE** *(a) Est-ce que technique* Est-ce que j' *ai donné ? Est-ce que tu* as donné ? *etc.*
(b) T.A.T. (Turn around technique) Est-ce que je* donne ?[1] *donnes-tu? *donne-*t*-il ? (elle)[2] *donnons-nous? *donnez-vous? *donnent-ils ? (elles)	*(b) T.A.T.* *ai-je donné? *as-tu donné? *a-*t*-il (elle) donné? *avons-nous donné ? *avez-vous donné? *ont-ils (elles) donné?
4. INTERROGATIVE NEGATIVE *(a) Est-ce que & 'sandwich'* Est-ce que je NE* donne PAS? Est-ce que tu NE* donnes PAS? etc *(b) 'T.A.T.' & 'sandwich'* Est-ce que je NE* donne PAS ? NE donnes-tu PAS? etc. NE donne-*t*-il PAS? etc.	**4. INTERROGATIVE NEGATIVE** *(a) Est-ce que & 'sandwich'* Est-ce que je N* ai PAS donné? Est-ce que tu N* as PAS donné? *(b) 'T.A.T.' & 'sandwich'* N*ai-je PAS donné? N*as-tu PAS donné? N*a-*t*-il PAS donné? etc.
* shows the position of any Object Pronoun	

NOTE 1:
  TAT is not normally used in the **je** form except in short,
     common verbs e.g. ai-je? suis-je?   puis-je?   etc.

NOTE 2:
  Remember the *hyphen-tee-hyphen* in the il and elle forms of the TAT method,
  to separate a verb ending in a vowel from the il and elle: porte-*t*-il? aimera-*t*-elle?
  donna-*t*-il?

NOTE 3:
  Noun as subject in TAT - state the noun and sum up in pronoun form
  Les élèves sont-ils dans la classe?
  Maman est-elle contente?

§39. IMPERATIVE   COMMAND FORM

1. Meaning
Negative

(a) Open!	←——— 2nd Person Singular ———→	Don't Open!
(b) Open!	←——— 2nd Person Plural ———→	Don't Open!
(c) Let us open!	←——— 1st Person Plural ———→	Don't let's open!

2. Formation

(a) Take the appropriate form of the verb:

2nd Sing : (Tu)	portes*	finis	vends	vas*	ne bois pas
2nd Plur : (Vous)	portez	finissez	vendez	allez	ne buvez pas
1st Plur : (Nous)	portons	finissons	vendons	allons	ne buvons pas
	"-er"	"-ir"	"-re"	Irregular	Negative

(b) Remove the Subject Pronouns

(c) *Remove the s in the *tu* form of -er verbs
(also aller, ouvrir, cueillir and compounds) But note that vas-y (= go on then!) retains the s for the sake of the sound.

(d) Exceptions

être	:	sois!	soyez!	soyons!	=	Be! Be! Let's be!
avoir	:	aie!	ayez!	ayons!	=	Have! Have! Let's have!
savoir	:	sache!	sachez!	sachons!	=	Know! Know! Let's Know!

3. Imperative with One Object Pronoun

(a) Reflexive Imperative

AFFIRMATIVE

Attach the Pronouns with a hyphen

lave - toi!   = wash (yourself)!
lavez-vous!   = wash (yourself)!
lavons-nous! = Lets's wash (ourselves)!
(*Note:* te becomes **toi**)

NEGATIVE

Place Pronoun before the verb. Enclose with a Negative Sandwich

Ne te lave pas!   = Don't wash!
Ne vous lavez pas!   = Don't wash!
Ne nous lavons pas! = Don't let's wash!
(*Note:* **toi** back to te)

(b) Other Imperatives with one object pronoun

AFFIRMATIVE

Attach the Pronoun with a hyphen

Mange - le!   = Eat it !
Poussez-moi!   = Push me!
MangEons - les! = Let's eat them!

(*Note* that me becomes **moi**)

NEGATIVE

Pronoun before verb. Negative Sandwich

Ne le mange pas!   = Don't eat it!
Ne me poussez pas!   = Don't push me!
Ne les mangEons pas = Don't let's eat them!

(*Note:* **moi** back to me)

4. Imperative with more than one Object Pronoun

AFFIRMATIVE
- *Attach the Pronouns with a hyphen*
- *Same order as in English (usually)*
- **moi & toi**, not *me & te*

NEGATIVE
- *Pronouns before verb. Negative Sandwich*
- *Order as the football team*
- **me & te**, not *moi & toi*

Examples

Donnez-le-moi!	**Ne** me le donnez **pas!**
= Give it (to) me!	= Don't give it (to) me!
Envoyez-les-lui!	**Ne** les lui envoyez **pas!**
= Send them to { him! her	= Don't send them (to) { him! her

5. *Tu* Form

When the *tu* form is being used in the conversation, remember to use the *tu* form Imperative.

E.g.
Aide-moi, s'il **te** plaît, **tu** es plus fort que moi.
= Help me, please, you are stronger than me.

Compare: Aidez-moi, s'il **vous** plaît, **vous** êtes plus fort que moi.

§ 40. IMPERSONAL VERBS

The subject is always *il*
Il y a; il pleut; il faut; il fait beau; il vaut mieux = it is better.
Il s'agit de = it is a matter of, it concerns: Il s'agit de mon mariage.

Some take an Indirect Object Pronoun:
Il ne **me** reste que trois jours = I have only three days left.
Il **lui** arrive très peu de bonheur = Very little happiness befalls him.
Il **me** semble qu'il a tort = It seems to me that he is wrong.

§41. INFINITIVES

— How to link infinitives to verbs, nouns, and adjectives.

1. Direct link

(a) *Common examples*

adorer	= to adore	faire	= to do, make
aimer	= to like, love	falloir	= to have to
aimer mieux	= to prefer	laisser	= to allow (to leave)
aller	= to go	oser	= to dare
compter	= to intend, expect	pouvoir	= to be able (can)
désirer	= to want, desire	préférer	= to prefer
détester	= to hate	savoir	= to know
devoir	= to have to	sembler	= to seem
espérer	= to hope	valoir mieux	= to be better
faillir	= to 'nearly'	vouloir	= to wish, want

Je préfère partir = I prefer to go
Je n'ose pas le faire
= I dare not do it

Il a failli mourir = He nearly died
Il vaudrait mieux partir
= It would be better to leave

(b) *Verbs of motion*

aller = to go (and)   Je vais le voir tous les jours.
envoyer = to send   J'envoie chercher le médecin.
venir = to come (and)   Je viens voir Jean.

(c) *Verbs of hearing and seeing*

entendre = to hear. Je l'ai entendu(e) chuchoter = I heard him whispering.
voir = to see. Je l'ai vu(e) manger.   (her)

Note: *entendre dire que* = to hear(tell) that:
J'ai entendu dire qu'il est parti = I have heard that he has gone.
    entendre parler de = to hear (speak) of.
Il a entendu parler de moi = He has heard of me.

Note these special constructions with faire

— *To make someone do something:*
   Je le fais pleurer = I make him weep

— *To have something done:*
   Il a fait réparer son auto = He had his car repaired.
   faire bâtir = to have built   se faire couper les cheveux = to have one's hair cut.
   faire cuire = to cook
   faire entrer = to show in

2. Linked by à

aider à	= to help to	se décider à	= to decide to
apprendre à	= to teach to (learn)	encourager à	= to encourage to
arriver à	= to manage to	hésiter à	= to hesitate to
s'attendre à	= to expect to	inviter à	= to invite to
avoir à	= to have to	se mettre à	= to begin to
chercher à	= to seek to	passer le temps à	= to spend the time doing
commencer à	= to begin to	se préparer à	= to prepare to
consentir à	= to consent to	réussir à	= to succeed in
continuer à	= to continue to	tarder à	= to be long in
beaucoup à	= a lot to	lent à	= slow to
bon à	= good to	lourd à	= heavy to
le dernier à	= the last to	mauvais à	= bad to
difficile à	= difficult to	occupé à	= busy (doing)
facile à.	= easy to	le premier à	= the first to
impossible à	= impossible to	prêt à	= ready to
léger à	= light to	quelque chose à	= something to
		rien à	= nothing to

Je commence à travailler = I begin to work.
Elle est prête à partir = She is ready to leave.

3. Linked by de

s'arrêter de	= to stop doing	finir de	= to finish doing
avoir besoin de	= to need to	offrir de	= to offer to
avoir peur de	= to be afraid to	oublier de	= to forget to
cesser de	= to stop doing	prier de	= to beg to
décider de	= to decide to	promettre de	= to promise to
essayer de	= to try to	refuser de	= to refuse to
empêcher de	= to prevent (from)	regretter de	= to regret doing
être obligé de	= to be obliged to	tâcher de	= to try to

certain de	= certain to	heureux de	= happy to
content de	= pleased (glad) to	obligé de	= obliged to
le désir de	= the desire to	l'occasion de	= the chance to
le droit de	= the right to	la permission de	= the permission to
enchanté de	= delighted to	le temps de	= the time to
étonné de	= astonished to		

Il essaie de traverser la rue. Je suis obligé de finir.
Il est certain de réussir. Je n'ai pas le temps de le faire.

4. à + person, de + Infinitive.

conseiller	à	quelqu'un de faire quelque chose	=	to advise someone to
demander	à	de	=	to ask someone to
défendre	à	de	=	to forbid someone to
dire	à	de	=	to tell someone to
ordonner	à	de	=	to order someone to
permettre	à	de	=	to permit someone to
persuader	à	de	=	to persuade someone to
promettre	à	de	=	to promise someone to

J'ai demandé à Jean de fermer la porte = I asked John to close the door.
Je lui ai demandé de la fermer = I asked him to close it. (Pronoun form)

5. Linked by pour = in order to (*implying a sense of purpose*)

Il s'est arrêté pour acheter un journal
   = He stopped (in order) to buy a newspaper.
Note: assez + adjective + **pour**   trop + adjective + **pour**
      assez âgé **pour** comprendre   trop fatigué **pour** courir

6. Introduced by other prepositions

sans, avant de, au lieu de, par. *See the following Section.*

§42. -ING ... HOW TO TRANSLATE

1. By an infinitive

   (a) **after certain prepositions.**

sans	= without	: sans travailler	= without working.
avant de	= before	: avant de manger	= before eating.
au lieu de	= instead of	: au lieu de partir	= instead of leaving.
par	= by	: used after verbs of beginning and finishing.	

Elle a commencé par pleurer = She began by crying.
Nous avons fini par comprendre la réalité = We finished by understanding the reality.

   (b) **after main verbs ...** (See Section 41)
J'aime manger = I like eating.
Il a réussi à ouvrir la porte = He succeeded in opening the door.
Il a commencé à pleuvoir = It began raining.

2. Perfect Infinitive

(a) **Avoir type**:

Après avoir mangé le gâteau = After eating the cake (= having eaten)
Après les avoir mangés = After having eaten them.
(*Note also*: Ayant mangé = Having eaten . . .)

(b) **Être type**:

Après être* arrivée à la gare, elle . . . = Having arrived at the station, she . . .
       rentrés à la maison, nous . . . = Having returned home, we . . .
          May be omitted.

(c) **Reflexive type**:

Après s' être levée, elle est partie = Having got up, she left.

3. By Present Participle.

Remove the *-ons* from the *nous* form of the present tense. Add the ending -ant.

e.g.: Nous travaill(ons) . . . becomes travaillant = working.
      Nous croy(ons) . . . becomes croyant = believing/thinking.
      Nous mangE(ons) . . . becomes mangeant = eating
      Exceptions: Avoir   . . .   **ayant** = having
               Être   . . .   **étant** = being
               Savoir   . . .   **sachant** = knowing

(a) *Present Participle standing alone:*
Elle était assise, **pleurant** = She was sitting, crying.

(b) *Present Participle + EN* . . . implies simultaneous actions, and means by/in/while/on doing something:
En écoutANT, il ouvrit la fenêtre = WHILE[1] listening, he opened the window
En étudiANT, on apprend bien = BY studying, you learn well

Note: **En courant** + descendre, monter, sortir.

J'ai* descendu l'escalier *en courant* = I *ran down* the stairs
Il a* monté l'escalier *en courant* = He *ran up* the stairs
Elle est sortie du cinéma *en courant* = She *ran out* of the cinema

(*See Section 6.B.III.2)

(c) *Present Participle + TOUT EN* . . . implies even greater simultaneity
Tout en causant, elle tricotait une chaussette.
= While chatting, she knitted a sock.

Note 1: Pendant que + Imperfect = while; Tandis que + Imperfect = whereas.
Pendant qu'il écoutait, il ouvrit la fenêtre.
Jean jouait, tandis que Claude travaillait. (Contrast is implied).

Note 2: Agreement of present participle?

(a) *Verbal sense* – **No** agreement
Elle est arrivée, en pleurant = She arrived, crying.
Elle s'est levée, en riant = She got up, laughing.

(b) *Adjectival sense*   **Agreement with the noun**
sa femme charmant**E** = his charming wife
les visages souriant**S** = the smiling faces

4. **By past participle**, when defining state or position. Agreement + Subject,

Je l'ai vu . . . assis(e)   = sitting   couché = lying
              agenouillé = kneeling   étendu = lying (stretched out)
              endormi   = sleeping   accoudé = leaning (on elbows)
              pendu   = hanging   adossé = leaning (back supported)
                                        appuyé = leaning (on a support)
              (Remember être **debout** = to be **standing** does not agree)

5. **Note these examples using an Infinitive.**

   Elle a passé la soirée à tricoter = She spent the evening knitting.
   J'aime nager = I like swimming.

6. **Basic French Tense for the English Continuous Tenses.**

Present:	I carry/do carry	am carry**ING**	=	je porte.
Future:	He will carry	will be carry**ING**	=	il portera.
Imperfect:	I carried/used to carry	was carry**ING**	=	je portais
Perfect:	I have carried	have been carry**ING**	=	j'ai porté

	Continuous	*Basic*
	English	*French*
	Tense	*Tense*

Note.
Être en train de + Infinitive = To be in the process of doing, implies further continuity:

Il est *en train de faire* ses devoirs = He $\begin{cases} is\ doing \\ is\ in\ the\ process\ of\ doing\ his\ homework. \end{cases}$

J'étais *en train de* déménager = I was removing
                                     was in the process of removing
                                     (= moving house)

7. **Qui + Imperfect.**

   I saw the men *working*
   = J'ai vu les hommes *qui travaillaient*

§43. INVERSION — When & Why?

1. **Interrogative Form (Turn Around Technique)**
   suis - je? = am I?
   donne - t -il? = does he give?

2. **After Direct Speech:**
   'Bonjour', a-t-elle dit (*or* a dit Hélène)
   'Il est arrivé', ajouta Jean

3. **When the following words begin a sentence:**

   Peut-être = *perhaps* :   **Peut-être** viendra-t-elle
                              = Perhaps she will come

   Add *QUE*, no inversion . . . **Peut-être QU'** elle viendra
   At the end, no inversion . . . Elle viendra, **peut-être**

Aussi/Ainsi = *so* (*therefore*)	Aussi est-il parti/Ainsi est-il parti. = So he left
toujours est-il que = *nevertheless*	Toujours est-il qu'elle est contente = Nevertheless she is happy
à peine = *hardly*	À peine fut-elle arrivée . . . Hardly had she arrived . . .

§44. MOTHER, FATHER, RELATIONS

Remember to qualify the noun with le/la, mon/ma, etc.
Ma mère a dit = Mother said . . .
But: Maman a dit   = Mum said
Mon père est arrivé = Father has arrived
But: Papa est arrivé   = Dad has arrived

    La tante Hélène est venue = Aunt Helen has come (See Section 26, Articles)

§45. NEGATIVES

1. **Negative "Sandwiches"** . . . these "Sandwiches" enclose:

   (a) *The Verb*   Je **ne** mange **pas**
   (b) *Any Object Pronouns*   Je **ne** *le* mange **pas** /Je **ne** *me* lève **pas**
   (c) *Subject Pronouns in Interrogatives*
      Ne mangez-*vous* **pas**?
      Ne *le* mangez-*vous* **pas**?

   (d) **Note: these rules hold good even in the perfect tense** (See Section 38)
      Je **ne** *vous les* ai **pas** . . . donnés. (Past Participle LAST)

ne . . . pas	= not	ne . . . guère	= hardly
ne . . . jamais	= never	ne . . . pas du tout	= not at all
ne . . . plus	= { no more/longer { not any more	ne . . . ni . . . ni	= neither . . . nor
ne . . . rien	= { nothing { not anything	ne . . . aucun(e) } ne . . . nul(le) }	= not any, no.
ne . . . personne	= nobody	ne . . . nulle part	= nowhere
ne . . . point	= not (rare)		
ne . . . que	= **ONLY**		

      Je **ne** mange **rien** = I eat nothing (not anything)
      Il **n'a ni** livres **ni** cahiers = He has neither books nor exercise books
      Je **n' ai que** deux francs = I have **only** two francs *-
      Elle **ne** parle **jamais** = She never speaks.
      Il **ne** mange **plus** = He eats no more/longer.
      Je **n'ai aucune** idée = I have not any/no idea
      (* *or* j'ai **seulement** deux francs)

2. **Exceptions to the "Sandwich" positioning technique**

(*In Compound Tenses only*)

Je n'ai vu **personne**   = I $\begin{cases} \text{have not seen anybody} \\ \text{have seen nobody} \end{cases}$

Je ne les ai vus **nulle part** = I $\begin{cases} \text{have not seen them anywhere} \\ \text{have seen them nowhere} \end{cases}$

Je n'ai mangé **que** du pain = I only ate some bread

3. **Rien (ne) and Personne (ne)** as the subject of the verb.

Rien ne tombe = Nothing falls   (no *pas*)
Personne ne parle = Nobody speaks   (no *pas*)

4. **Personne, rien and jamais standing alone**

Qui est arrivé? – **Personne!**   = Who has arrived? – Nobody!
Qu'est-ce qu'il a écrit? – **Rien!** = What has he written? – Nothing!
As-tu jamais lu ce livre ? – **Jamais!**= Have you ever read this book ?
                                  – Never !

5. **Negatives with the Infinitive**: use **ne pas**, etc.

   – Je lui ai ordonné de **ne pas** parler (= *not to speak*)
   – Elle a décidé de **ne rien** manger (= *to eat nothing*)
   – Ils m'ont demandé de **ne jamais** parler (= *. . . to never speak*)

6. **Two Negatives Combined** (arrange them in alphabetical order)

   – Je ne fais **plus rien**   = I no longer do anything
   – Je ne lui donne **jamais rien** = I never give (to) him anything
     Nous n'y allions **jamais plus** = We never went there any more

7. **Negative questions and statements;** *si* means *yes*

N'a-t-il pas fini ? - *SI*   = Hasn't he finished ? - Yes
Ce n'est pas cher ! - *SI*, c'est cher !
= It isn't dear ! - Yes, it's dear !

8. **N'est-ce pas?** - an invariable phrase.

Tu es content . . . . **n'est-ce pas?**   *aren't you?*
Elle l'a fait . . . . **n'est-ce pas?**   *hasn't she?*
Nous serons à temps . . **n'est-ce pas?**   *won't we?*

9. **Non plus (n) either**
Je ne le ferai pas **non plus** = I shall not do it *either*
Moi **non plus** = *Neither* shall I.

§46. NUMBERS

1. Numbers 0–100

0	**zéro**
1	un (une)
2	deux
3	trois
4	quatre
5	cinq
6	six
7	sept
8	huit
9	neuf
10	**dix**
11	onze
12	douze
13	treize
14	quatorze
15	quinze
16	seize
17	dix-sept
18	dix-huit
19	dix-neuf
20	**vingt**
21	vingt et un
22	vingt-deux
23	vingt-trois
24	vingt-quatre
25	vingt-cinq
26	vingt-six
27	vingt-sept
28	vingt-huit
29	vingt-neuf
30	**trente**
31	trente et un
32	trente-deux
33	trente-trois
34	trente-quatre
35	trente-cinq
36	trente-six
37	trente-sept
38	trente-huit
39	trente-neuf
40	**quarante**
41	quarante et un
42	quarante-deux
43	quarante-trois
44	quarante-quatre
45	quarante-cinq
46	quarante-six
47	quarante-sept
48	quarante-huit
49	quarante-neuf
50	**cinquante**
51	cinquante et un
52	cinquante-deux
53	cinquante-trois
54	cinquante-quatre
55	cinquante-cinq
56	cinquante-six
57	cinquante-sept
58	cinquante-huit
59	cinquante-neuf
60	**soixante**
61	soixante et un
62	soixante-deux
63	soixante-trois
64	soixante-quatre
65	soixante-cinq
66	soixante-six
67	soixante-sept
68	soixante-huit
69	soixante-neuf
70	**soixante-dix**
71	soixante et onze
72	soixante-douze
73	soixante-treize
74	soixante-quatorze
75	soixante-quinze
76	soixante-seize
77	soixante-dix-sept
78	soixante-dix-huit
79	soixante-dix-neuf
80	**quatre-vingts**
81	quatre-vingt-un
82	quatre-vingt-deux
83	quatre-vingt-trois
84	quatre-vingt-quatre
85	quatre-vingt-cinq
86	quatre-vingt-six
87	quatre-vingt-sept
88	quatre-vingt-huit
89	quatre-vingt-neuf
90	**quatre-vingt-dix**
91	quatre-vingt-onze
92	quatre-vingt-douze
93	quatre-vingt-treize
94	quatre-vingt-quatorze
95	quatre-vingt-quinze
96	quatre-vingt-seize
97	quatre-vingt-dix-sept
98	quatre-vingt-dix-huit
99	quatre-vingt-dix-neuf
100	**cent**

2. Numbers above 100.

101	cent un	**Idiomatic phrases**
102	cent deux (etc)	Mille et Une* Nuits
110	cent dix (etc)	= 1001 Nights (= Arabian Nights)
111	cent onze (etc)	**Mille et Un Points**
200	deux cents	= 1001 points (many or countless)
201	deux cent un	*Mille un* means *exactly* 1001
1000	mille	
1001	mille un	*Note the agreement.*
2000	deux mille	*Note also* cinq milles = five miles
1,000,000	= un million (de)	

3. Ordinal Numbers: basic rule: Add -ième.

1st	premier (première)		8th	huitième
2nd	second(e) or deuxième		9th	neuvième ($f \rightarrow v$)
3rd	troisième		10th	dixième
4th	quatrième (drop e)		11th	onzième (etc. drop e)
5th	cinqUième (add u)		20th	vingtième
6th	sixième		21st	vingt et unième
7th	septième			

4. Note these expressions in -aine

une douzaine de pommes	=	a dozen apples
une quinzaine de jours	=	a fortnight
une vingtaine d'hommes	=	20 or so men
des centaines de soldats	=	hundreds of soldiers
And: des milliers de voitures	=	thousands of cars

-aine indicates an approximate number.

§47. ONE OF . . .

	Un (e) de mes ami(e)s	= one of my (female) friends
	L'un d'entre eux	= one of them (m.)
	L'une d'entre elles	= one of them (f.)
Also:	Un ami médecin	= A doctor friend . . .

§48. THE PARTITIVE ARTICLE

Du
De la
De l'   } = some *, or any
Des
De   *often omitted in English
D'

I eat _____ cakes

I like _____ oranges

M.S. DE + LE = DU	J'ai *DU* pain	= (I have some bread (I have —— bread
	Avez-vous *DU* pain?	= Have you any bread?
F.S. DE + LA = DE LA	J'ai *DE LA* salade	= (I have some salad (I have —— salad
	As-tu *DE LA* salade	= Have you any salad?
M.S. before vowel DE + L' = DE L'	Je mange *DE L*'ail	= (I eat some garlic (I eat —— garlic
	Avez-vous *DE L*'ail?	= Have you any garlic?
F.S. before vowel DE + L' = DE L'	Je bois *DE L*'eau	= (I drink some water (I drink —— water
	Bois-tu *DE L*'eau?	= Do you drink any water?
M.P. DE + LES = DES	Je mange *DES* gâteaux	= (I eat some cakes (I eat —— cakes
	Mangez-vous *DES* gâteaux	= Do you eat any cakes?
F.P. DE + LES = DES	Je mange *DES* pommes	= (I eat some apples (I eat —— apples
	Mangez-vous *DES* pommes?	= Do you eat any apples?

DE is used alone in certain cases:

(a) **After a negative** (*exception*: NE . . . QUE = only, see note 3)

    — Elle NE mange PLUS **DE PAIN**
       = She doesn't eat bread any longer
    — Elle NE mange JAMAIS **DE** viande
       = She never eats any meat
    — Il N'a PAS **DE** stylos
       = He hasn't (any) pens

Note 1: NOT A = PAS DE
              Je n'ai PAS DE stylo = I haven't a pen

Note 2: PAS UN = NOT A SINGLE
              Je n'ai PAS UN billet = I haven't a single note

Note 3: NE . . . QUE
              Je NE mange QUE DU pain = I only eat bread

(b) **Immediately before a plural adjective**

    — Nous voyons **DE JOLIES** maisons
       = We see (some) pretty houses
    — Il m'a donné **DE PETITS** bonbons rouges
       = He gave me (some) little red sweets

Remember: J'ai d'autres choses à faire = I have other things to do.
(*But:* **DES** jeunes gens = young people, **DES** petits pois = peas; The *De alone* rule does not apply to these common compounded units).

(c) **After words of quantity**

(beaucoup **D**' argent	= much money
(beaucoup **D**' allumettes	= many, a lot of, matches
(*But:* bien **DES**	= much, many, a lot)
(trop **D**' oeufs	= too many eggs)
(trop **D**' eau	= too much water)
(tant **DE** bruit	= so much noise)
(tant **DE** gens	= so many people)
un peu **DE** viande*	= a little (=some) meat
combien **DE** stylos?	= how many pens?
(autant **DE** fromage . . . que	= as much cheese as
(autant **DE** stylos . . . que	= as many pens as
assez **DE** fromage	= enough cheese
moins **D**' argent	= less money

But: **La plupart** *des* + **plural verb** = Most of
La plupart *des* élèves **sont** jeunes = Most of the pupils are young
(*See Sec.36, A few . . . some)

(d) **After containers and measures**

Une boîte **DE** sardines	= a tin of sardines
Un paquet **DE** bonbons	= a packet of sweets
Un kilo **DE** fromage	= a kilo of cheese
Une livre **DE** farine	= a pound of flour

§49. THE PASSIVE VOICE

1. **Formation: Être + Past Participle,** *which agrees with the Subject*

Present : La locomotive *est* venduE	= the locomotive is sold
Perfect : Elle *a été* vendue	= It has been sold
Past Hist. : Elle *fut* vendue	= It was sold (event))
Imperfect : Elle *était* vendue	= It was sold (state)) *See Note below.

Future	: Elle *sera* vendue	= It will be sold
Conditional	: Elle *serait* vendue	= It would be sold
Fut. Perfect	: Elle *aura été* vendue	= It will have been sold
Condit. Perfect	: Elle *aurait été* vendue	= It would have been sold
Pluperfect	: Elle *avait été* vendue	= It had been sold

Note also Il *a été* blessé = He was wounded (**event**) at 10 o'clock.
à dix heures
Il *était* blessé = He was wounded (**state**)

2. **How to avoid the Passive in French**

(a) **You may use** *on*

.On a trouvé votre livre	= Your book *has been* found
On dit qu'il est fou	= *It is said* that he is mad
On sait que . . .	= *It is* known that . . .
On croit que . . .	= *It is* (believed) that, . . . (thought)

(b) **You may use the Reflexive**

Je M'appelle Jean   = I **am** called Jean
Ce mot ne S'emploie pas = This word **is** not used
Les poires SE vendent ici = Pears **are** sold here

§50. PERFECT INFINITIVE

1. See Section 42, No. 2. (*après avoir mangé*, etc.)

2. Other examples

— Je suis étonné d'*être tombé*   )
  = I am astonished to **have** fallen) Être type
— Je suis heureux d'*avoir gagné*)
  = I am happy to **have** won   ) Avoir type

§51. PLURALS OF NOUNS

1. **ending in -s, -x, -z: no change**
   voice: la voix   les voix

2. **ending in -eau change to -eaux**
   cloak: le manteau   les manteaux

3. **ending in -al change to -aux**
   newspaper: le journal   les journaux

4. **ending in -eu change to -eux**
   fire: le feu   les feux
   (Exception: tyre: le pneu   les pneus

5. **ending in -ou change to -ous**
   hole: le trou   les trous
   Exceptions les cailloux = pebbles   les bijoux = jewels
                les genoux = knees   les choux = cabbages
                les hiboux = owls

	Compare Plural Adjectives
	Section 21B
	beau - be*aux*
	général - génér*aux*
	hébreu - hébr*eux*
	bleu - bleu*s*)

6. **Compound nouns**

grandparent	le grand-parent	les grands-parents
grandmother	la grand-mère	les grand-mères
grandfather	le grand-père	les grands-pères
father-in-law	le beau-père	les beaux-pères
mother-in-law	la belle-mère	les belles-mères
brother-in-law	le beau-frère	les beaux-frères

7. **Note also**

monsieur	**mes**sieurs	l'oeil	les yeux (eyes)
madame	**mes**dames	le ciel	les cieux
mademoiselle	**mes**demoiselles	(sky)	(heavens)

§52. POUVOIR/VOULOIR/SAVOIR & CONNAÎTRE

1. **Pouvoir** = *to be able, to can*

Present	: Il peut venir	= He *can* (= is able to) come
(**Imperfect**	: Je pouvais aller	= I could (= *was able*) to go
(**Conditional**	: Je pourrais aller	= I could (= *would be able to/might*) go

Note 1: Use *puis-je?* (= may I?) in the TAT interrogative form.

Note 2: Pouvoir is often omitted with verbs of seeing and hearing
I can see the house = Je **vois** la maison
We could hear the noise = Nous **entendions** le bruit
    (= *were able*)

Note 3: Difference between Pouvoir and Savoir
Pouvoir is to be **P**hysically capable
Il peut nager = He can swim (i.e. his leg injury has been cured)
Savoir is to know how (to have the *'savvy'* or skill)
Il sait nager = He can swim (because he has learned to)

2. **Vouloir**

Vouloir means *will/would* in senses other than the future (e.g. requests)
e.g. Voulez-vous le faire? = *Will* you do it? (=are you willing to do it ?)
    Je ne voulais pas le faire = I *would* not do it (= was unwilling to do it)

3. **Savoir** is *to know facts*

Je sais qu'elle est malade = I know that she is ill

Connaître *is to know people and places*
Je connais bien Paris (Hélène). = I know Paris (Helen) well.

§53. PREPOSITIONS

1. **Built into the French**

apercevoir	= to catch sight **of**		envoyer chercher	= to send **for**
attendre	= to wait **for**		indiquer	= to point **to**
chercher	= to look **for**		montrer	= to point **to**
demander	= to ask **for**		payer	= to pay **for**
écouter	= to listen **to**		regarder	= to look **at**

J'écoute la radio. Je paye le billet.

2. **à before the noun** *(or pronoun)*

acheter à	= to buy (from)	nuire à	= to harm
assister à	= to attend, watch	obéir à	= to obey
s'attendre à	= to expect	penser à	= to think of (dream)
demander à	= to ask (from person)	(penser de	= to think of (opinion))
emprunter à	= to borrow (from pers.)	plaire à	= to please

faire mal à	= to hurt		renoncer à	= to give up
se fier à	= to trust		répondre à	= to answer
s'intéresser à	= to be interested in		résister à	= to resist
jouer à	= to play (sports)		ressembler à	= to look like
(jouer de	= to play instruments)		voler à	= to steal (from person)

J'ai volé un stylo à Jean. J'ai assisté au match de football.
Je m'intéresse à la musique. Il résiste à la tentation

3. de before the noun (or pronoun)

s'approcher de	= to approach		se moquer de	= to make fun of
avoir besoin de	= to need		s'occuper de	= to look after
avoir pitié de	= to pity		se passer de	= to do without
changer de	= to change		partir de	= to leave ___ (penser de)
se charger de	= to undertake		profiter de	= to take advantage of
dépendre de	= to depend on		rire de	= to laugh at
descendre de	= to get off (bus)		se servir de	= to use
se douter de	= to suspect		se souvenir de	= to remember
jouir de	= to enjoy		se tromper de	= to mistake (to get the thing
manquer de	= to lack			wrong)
se méfier de	= to distrust			

Je m'approche de lui. Tout dépend de moi. Je manque d'argent.
Il profite des circonstances. Je me trompe de chemin (no article used with se tromper de)

4. Others

entrer **dans**	= to enter	Il est entré dans la chambre.
monter **dans**	= to get on	Je suis monté dans l'autobus.
pénétrer **dans**	= to penetrate	Nous avons pénétré dans la forêt.
se diriger **vers**	= to make for	Nous nous dirigeons vers la ville.
compter **sur**	= to rely on	Je compte sur Jean.

§54. PUNCTUATION

.	point	= full stop
,	virgule	= comma
;	point-virgule	= semi-colon
:	deux points	= colon
?	point d'interrogation	= question mark
!	point d'exclamation	= exclamation mark
≪≫	guillemets	= quotation marks
—	tiret	= dash
-	trait d'union	= hyphen
...	points de suspension	= dots, suspension marks
( )	parenthèses	= brackets

§55. QUAND + FUTURE TENSE

Change the **Quand** clause as follows

1. **English Present ⟶ French Future**
   I shall finish when he *arrives*   Present (= will arrive)
   Je finirai quand il *arrivera*   Future

2. **English Perfect ⟶ French Future Perfect**
   I shall do it when he *has seen* it   Perfect (= will have seen it)
   Je le ferai quand il l'*aura vu*   Future Perfect

§56. REFLEXIVE VERBS

			Corresponds to
me	cacher = to hide	**myself**	*je*
te	cacher = to hide	**yourself**	*tu*
se	cacher = to hide	**him/her/one/self**	*il/elle/on*
nous	cacher = to hide	**ourselves**	*nous*
vous	cacher = to hide	**yourselves**	*vous*
se	cacher = to hide	**themselves**	*ils/elles*

Non-Reflexive

		Reflexive	
Je cache	**le livre**	Je **me** cache	= I hide (myself)
Je lève	**le bras**	Je **me** lève	= I get (myself) up
Il arrête	**le voleur**	Il s' arrête	= He stops (himself)
Tu réveilles	**l'enfant**	Tu **te** réveilles	= You wake (yourself) up
Nous lavons	**le jouet**	Nous **nous** lavons	= We wash (ourselves)

|Direct Object| |Direct Object Reflexive Pronoun|

Note 1: *Reciprocal Meaning of Reflexives*

   Nous nous aimons   = We love *each other*
   Ils s'envoient des lettres = They send *each other* letters
   Ils se regardent   = They look at *each other*

Note 2:
   La porte s'est ouverte = The door opened   (Person **unknown**)
   Il a ouvert la porte   = He opened the door (Person known)
   La porte s'est fermée = The door closed   (Person **unknown**)
   Il a fermé la porte   = He closed the door (Person known)

§57. REPETITION

1. **Articles** - repeat

   le garçon et **la** jeune fille = the boy and —— girl
   du café et **du** sucre   = some coffee and —— sugar

2. **Possessive Adjectives** - repeat

   ma soeur et **mon** frère = my sister and —— brother

3. **Prepositions linking infinitives** - repeat

   J'ai décidé de prendre l'autobus et **de** visiter le musée
   = I decided to catch the bus and to visit the museum

4. When is not repeated in the same sentence

for quand or lorsque, use instead *que*
Quand j'ai fini, et *que* je me suis levé . . .
When I finished and when I got up . . .

§58. SI AND ITS MEANINGS

1. **If**: s'il réussit, cela m'étonnera = If he succeeds, that will astonish me.

2. **Yes** in answer to a negative question or statement.
   'N'as-tu pas fini?' — 'Si!' 'Tu n'iras pas!' — 'Si, j'irai!'

3. **Whether** - see section on si clauses.

4. **So + adjective**: il est si grand qu'il ne peut pas y entrer.

5. **as in negative comparatives**
   il n'est pas (*aus-*) si grand que moi. (See Section 31)

6. **Such + adjective**: Il a une si grande voiture. (See Section 64)

§59. SI CLAUSES

1. **Meaning 'if'** *same tense as in English.*

	Present	Future
S' = If	il pleut it rains	je *resterai* chez moi I shall stay at home
	Imperfect	**Conditional**
S' = If S' = If	il pleuvait it rained il venait he came	je *resterais* à la maison I would stay at home Je le *verrais* I would see him
	Pluperfect	**Conditional Perfect**
Si = If	l'homme était venu the man had come	je l'*aurais vu* I would have seen him

2. **Meaning 'whether'** *future or conditional may be used.*

    Je me demande s'il *réussira*.
= I wonder whether he will succeed.
    Je me demandais s'il *viendrait*.
= I wondered)
   was wondering) whether he would come.

§60. SITTING/STANDING

1. Sitting

Action –	je m'assieds	= I sit down	**(Present)**
Reflexive	je me suis assis(e)	= I sat down	**(Perfect)**
State –	je suis assis(e)	= I am sitting	**(Present)**
être + adj.	j'étais assis(e)	= I was sitting	**(Imperfect)**

2. Standing

Action –	je me lève	= I stand (up)	**(Present)**
Reflexive	je me suis levé	= I stood (up)	**(Perfect)**
State –	je suis debout*	= I am standing	**(Present)**
être + adj.	j'étais debout*	= I was standing	**(Imperfect)**

No agreement.

Note also **se tenir** = to be standing.
e.g. Il se tenait au coin de la rue = He was standing at the corner of the street.

§61. 'SO' – HOW TO TRANSLATE INTO FRENCH

1. Therefore. Ainsi or aussi + Inversion or *donc* + affirmative

Ainsi/Aussi est-il descendu ⎫
    il est donc descendu   ⎬ = so he went down
                  ⎭

2. 'So' + adjective. (See Section 58.4).

§62. SUBJECT OF THE VERB *NOUS*

Ma soeur et moi, (= **Nous**) sommes allés au cinéma.
Note that with a subject of mixed gender, masculine takes precedence.
Thus the agreement is *-s* not *-es*.

§63. THE SUBJUNCTIVE MOOD

1. FORMATION OF THE SUBJUNCTIVE.

1. Present Subjunctive

(a) **Regular.**

Stem provided by 3rd person plural of the Present Indicative.

Present Indicative	Present Subjunctive
ils **finissent**	finisse, -es, -e, -ions, -iez, -ent,
ils **donnent**	donne, -es, -e, -ions, -iez, -ent,
ils **disent**	dise, -es, -e, -ions, -iez, -ent.

(b) Irregular

aller	aille, -es, -e; allions, alliez; aillent.
avoir	aie, aies, ait; ayons, ayez; aient.
être	sois, sois, soit; soyons, soyez; soient.
faire	fasse, -es, -e; fassions, -iez; fassent.
pouvoir	puisse, -es, -e; puissions, -iez; puissent.
savoir	sache, -es, -e; sachions, -iez; sachent.
valoir	vaille, -es, -e; valions, -iez; vaillent.
vouloir	veuille, -es, -e; voulions, -iez; veuillent.

(c) "Semi-irregular"

Derived from the 3rd person plural of the Present Indicative.
Nous and *vous* identical with the Imperfect Indicative; i.e. the stem change in the Present Indicative is maintained in the Present Subjunctive.

This applies to:

appeler	devoir	jeter	recevoir	voir
boire	envoyer	mourir	tenir	
croire	fuir	prendre	venir	

Present Indicative.	Imperfect Indicative.	Present Subjunctive.
Je viens	Je venais	Je **vienn**-e
tu viens	tu venais	tu **vienn**-es
il vient	il venait	il **vienn**-e
nous venons	nous **venions**	nous **ven-ions**
vous venez	vous **veniez**	vous **ven-iez**
ils **vienn**ent	ils venaient	ils **vienn**-ent

2. Imperfect Subjunctive

Always one of 4 types, depending on past historic types — *-ai, -is, -us,-ins.*

(a) -AI type

Je donnasse
tu donnasses
il donnât
nous donnassions
vous donnassiez
ils donnassent

(b) -IS type

Je vendisse
tu vendisses
il vendît
nous vendissions
vous vendissiez
ils vendissent

(c) -US type.......including avoir and être

Je reçusse	eusse	fusse
tu reçusses	eusses	fusses
il reçût	eût	fût
nous reçussions	eussions	fussions
vous reçussiez	eussiez	fussiez
ils reçussent	eussent	fussent

(d) -INS type

VENIR	TENIR
Je vinsse	Je tinsse
tu vinsses	tu tinsses
il vînt	il tînt
nous vinssions	nous tinssions
vous vinssiez	vous tinssiez
ils vinssent	ils tinssent

3. Perfect and Pluperfect Subjunctives.

Put the auxiliary (avoir or être) into the subjunctive:

Indicative		**Subjunctive**
vous avez vu	⟶	il faut que vous *ayez* vu
ils sont partis	⟶	avant qu'ils *soient* partis*
elle était arrivée	⟶	bien qu'elle *fût* arrivée*

*Note: that the formation and agreements of the Perfect and Pluperfect Subjunctive are similar to the Perfect and Pluperfect Indicative.

II. USAGE - Some common examples.

1. After vouloir que and other expressions of wishing and emotion, e.g.:

désirer que   préférer que   être content que = to be glad that
regretter que   aimer mieux que   être fâché que   = to be annoyed that
Je *veux que* tu m'**attendes** = I want you to wait for me
Il est *content que* nous **ayons** réussi = He is glad that we have succeeded.

2. After il faut que and il est nécessaire que

Il faut que je le **fasse** = I must do it
Il est nécessaire que nous **arrivions** à temps = we must arrive in time.

3. After certain conjunctions, e.g.:

avant que = before   pour que)
bien que)   afin que) = in order that
quoique) = although   pourvu que = provided that
jusqu'à ce que = until

Bien qu'il **soit** fatigué = Although he is tired
Je le ferai *avant que* tu **partes** = I shall do it before you leave
Je le ferai *jusqu'à ce qu*'il **arrive** = I will do it until he arrives
Note 1: attendre que = to wait until
J'attendrai que la salle **soit** libre = I shall wait until the hall is free.
Note 2: Not until = ne . . . que + lorsque (Indicative)
Nous ne commencerons que lorsque Jean se sera assis
= We shall not begin until John sits down.

4. After doubt, denial and possibility.

Je doute qu'il **soit** compétent = I doubt that he is competent
Il a nié qu'il l'**ait** volé = He denied that he has stolen it.
Il est possible que)
Il se peut que   ) tu **aies** raison = It is possible that you are right.
Il semble que vous **ayez** tort = It seems that you are wrong.
Note: the following take the Indicative:
      Il est probable que = It is probable that
      Il *me* semble que   = It seems to me that
            douter si   = to doubt whether.

5. After ordering, forbidding and requesting

J'ai ordonné que les voleurs **soient** emprisonnés
= I ordered that the thieves should be imprisoned
Je défends qu'on **passe** par là
= I forbid anybody to go that way
Il demande que je m'en **aille** = He asks that I go away.

6. **After a Superlative** (and dernier, premier, seul, meilleur)

C'est *le plus grand marteau que* j'**aie** jamais acheté
= It is the biggest hammer that I have ever bought
Voici *le seul bateau qui* **soit** arrivé
= Here is the only boat that has arrived

7. **After a non-specific antecedent**

Il est impossible de trouver *quelqu'un qui* **puisse** le faire
= It is impossible to find anybody who can do it
Est-ce qu'il y a *un médecin qui* **sache** le guérir?
= Is there a doctor who can (= knows how to) cure him?

8. **The untranslatable NE**

   (a) *After expressions of fearing*, e.g: avoir peur que, de peur que, craindre que,
   de crainte que.
   J'ai peur qu'ils **NE** m'arrêtent = I am afraid that they may arrest me
   Il ment de crainte qu'elle **NE** l'accuse
   He lies for fear that she may accuse him.

   (b) *After the conjunction à moins que = unless*
   À moins que nous **NE** le fassions maintenant
   = Unless we do it now

   (c) *After empêcher:* Empêchez qu'ils **NE** viennent! = Prevent them from coming!

   (d) *After ne (douter) pas que = to not doubt that*
   Je ne doute pas qu'il **N'**ait raison = I do not doubt that he is right.

9. **Avoidance of the Subjunctive**

   (a) *By an Infinitive* – when both clauses have the same subject.
   Je veux *attendre* = I want to wait
   Il est content d'*avoir réussi* = He is glad that he has succeeded
   Il me faut le *faire* = I must do it
   Je le ferai avant de *partir* = I shall do it before I leave.

   (b) *By a noun*
   Je le ferai avant $\begin{cases} \text{mon} \\ \text{ton} \end{cases}$ *départ* = I shall do it before $\begin{cases} \text{I} \\ \text{you} \end{cases}$ leave.

10. **Which tense of the Subjunctive?**

After conjunctions the tense is usually clear:
Quoiqu'il *soit* fatigué = Although he *is* tired
Bien qu'il *fût* fatigué = Although he *was* tired

The **Sequence of Tenses** is a guide to the tense of the Subjunctive in the Subordinate Clause.

Main Clause	Present Subjunctive	
Present . . . . Il faut $\big)$		I must drink it
Future . . . . Il faudra $\big\}$	que je le boive	I will have to drink it
Perfect + *have* . . Il a fallu $\big)$		I **have** had to drink it
Imperative . . . . Ordonnez	qu'il le boive!	Order him to drink it!

Main Clause	Imperfect Subjunctive
Imperfect ..... Il fallait	qu'il arrivât de bonne heure He had to (= used to have to) arrive early
Perfect .... Il a fallu *without have*	qu'il arrivât de bonne heure hier matin He had to arrive early yesterday morning
Past Historic ... Il fallut	qu'il arrivât de bonne heure la veille He had to arrive early the day before
Conditional · · · · Il faudrait	qu'il arrivât de bonne heure He would have to arrive early

In modern French, the cumbersome Imperfect Subjunctive is rarely used other than in the 3rd Person Singular.

§64. TEL = SUCH(A) + NOUN

Un tel soldat   = such a soldier
Une telle fleur = such a flower

de tels soldats = such soldiers
de telles fleurs = such flowers

Note: *Such + Adjective is si*

> Il a une *si* grande maison
> = He has such a large house
> Nous avons de *si* grandes voitures
> = We have such big cars

§65. THAT — HOW TO TRANSLATE INTO FRENCH

1. **Qui/Que** (Section 19)

   Voilà la voiture qui est chère
   = There's the car that is expensive

   Où est le livre que je viens d'acheter?
   = Where is the book that I have just bought?

2. **Cela (or Ça in speech)**   (Section 16)

   J'aime cela/ça = I like that

3. **Dont** (Section 19)

   Voici l'argent dont j'ai besoin
   = Here's the money that I (have) need (of)

4. Ce/cet/ces/cette (+ -là) (Section 15)

ce livre-là   = that (there!) book.
cette pomme-là = that (there!) apple.

5. celui/celle/celles/ceux (Section 16)

Celle de Jean est grande = That of John (i.e. John's) is large.

§66. TIME

1. Temps = time (non-specific)

Examples: Il est arrivé à temps = he arrived in time

J' attendais depuis longtemps (See Section 69)
Je n'ai pas le temps de le faire
= I haven't the time to do it

Note: Le temps = the weather (See Section 71)

2. L'heure

(a) = **hour:**   à toute heure du jour = at all hours of the day

(b) = **appointed time:**
l'heure du dîner = dinner time.
C'est l'heure!   = It's time!
être à l'heure   = to be on time

Note: Tout à l'heure = presently

(c) **Time by the clock**

Quelle heure est-il?   = What time is it?
Il est une heure   = It is 1 o'clock
Il est deux heures   = It is 2 o'clock
Il est midi   = It is 12 noon
Il est minuit   = It is 12 midnight
Il est trois heures et quart = It is 3.15
Il est cinq heures et demiE = It is 5.30   **(heure** is *feminine*)
Il est (midi) et demi   = It is 12.30   **(midi** and **minuit** are *masculine*)
   (minuit)
Il est sept heures moins (le quart = It is 6.45
                         (un

Il est dix heures dix   = It is 10.10
Il est dix heures moins dix   = It is 9.50

Un quart d'heure   = a quarter of an hour
Trois quarts d'heure = three quarters of an hour
Une demi-heure   = Half an hour

Nearly : Il est *près de* neuf heures, or, il est *presque* neuf heures
About   : *Vers* six heures, or *à* six heures *environ*
Exactly : à cinq heures *précises*
To strike : huit heures son*n*aient   Une heure sonna
             = 8 o'clock was striking = 1 o'clock struck.

a.m. : *du* matin
p.m. : *de l'*après-midi
p.m. : *du* soir

3. **Fois** = time = occasion

Je l'ai fait deux fois = I have done it two times (twice)

4. **Époque** = time = époque

à cette époque-là = At that time.....

5. **Matin/Matinée, etc.**

	Masculine	Feminine
year	un an	*une année*
morning	le matin	*la matinée*
evening	le soir	*la soirée*
day	le jour	*la journée*
	These above words often record the event	*These above words often imply a sense of duration*

(Le *Jour* de l'*an* = New Year's Day
(J'ai passé une *année* à apprendre le français

(Hier *matin*, je suis allé au marché
(Pendant la *matinée* j'ai fait des exercices

(Le *soir* il pleut beaucoup
(J'ai passé la *soirée* chez Hélène

(Il y a deux *jours* = two days ago ...
(Nous avons passé une belle *journée* chez lui

6. **Expressions of time**

dimanche matin	= (on) Sunday morning
demain (matin)	= tomorrow (morning)
après-demain	= the day after tomorrow
aujourd'hui	= today
hier (soir)	= yesterday (evening)
le lendemain	= the next day
le lendemain matin	= the next morning
la veille	= the previous day, eve
lundi	= on Monday
le lundi	= on Mondays
tous les lundis	= every Monday

§67. TOWNS/COUNTRIES/NATIONALITIES

1. **Le pays** = the Country

> **La langue** = language
> **l'habitant** = inhabitant
> **adjectif** = adjective

   (a) *Feminine*

France	= La France	français (e)
Great Britain	= La Grande-Bretagne	britannique
England	= L'Angleterre	anglais (e)
Scotland	= L'Écosse	écossais (e)
Ireland	= L'Irlande	irlandais (e)

Germany	= L'Allemagne	allemand (e)
Spain	= L'Espagne	espagnol (e)
Belgium	= La Belgique	belge
Holland	= La Hollande	hollandais (e)
Italy	= L'Italie	italien (ne)
Austria	= L'Autriche	autrichien (ne)
Switzerland	= La Suisse	suisse
Russia	= La Russie (L'U.R.S.S.)	russe
Australia	= L'Australie	australien (ne)
South Africa	= L'Afrique du Sud	sud-africain (e)
Europe	= L'Europe	européen (ne)
Asia	= L'Asie	asiatique
Czechoslovakia	= La Tchécoslovaquie	tchécoslovaque
New Zealand	= La Nouvelle-Zélande	néo-zélandais (e)

(b) *Masculine*

Wales	= Le Pays de Galles	gallois (e)
Portugal	= Le Portugal	portugais (e)
Canada	= Le Canada	canadien (ne)
United States	= Les États-Unis (m.pl)	américain (e)
Japan	= Le Japon	japonais

Capital letter or small letter?

(a) **Small letter**

    (i) *adjective:* e.g. un livre allemand = a German book
                  des danseuses espagnoles = (some) Spanish dancers

    (ii) *the language:* l'espagnol = Spanish
                  le français = French

Note the omission of the article

Parlez-vous espagnol? - Non, je parle français
But Je parle *bien le* portugais (*le* is used when an adverb is
introduced into the sentence)

(b) **Capital letters**

    (i) *The inhabitant*   Je vois trois Irlandaises
                        = I (can) see three Irish ladies

    (ii) *The Countries:*   La France, La Belgique

2. To/in/from with Countries

To and In with Feminine countries is **en**
e.g. Nous sommes allés en France.
From with Feminine countries is **de**
e.g. Je suis revenu d'Italie.

To and In with Masculine countries is **au**
e.g. Nous sommes allés au Japon (*Aux* États-Unis).
From with Masculine countries is **du**
e.g. Ils sont revenus du Canada (**des** États-Unis).

3. **To/at/in with Towns - use à**

Il est à Paris. Je vais à Londres.

4. **In a County - use dans le**

J'habite *dans le* Lancashire. **But**: *En* Bretagne (A French province).

§68. TU OR VOUS?

1. **When to 'tutoyer'** (= to use the *tu* form)

Familiar and Singular
To a friend, to a pet, to a child, to a family member.

2. **When to 'vouvoyer'** (=to use the *vous* form)

(a) *Polite - Singular* **and** *Plural*
to respected person(s), child to adult(s), to unknown person(s)etc.
(b) *Familiar and Plural*
    − to more than one friend, pet, child, family member.

§69. VENIR DE = TO HAVE JUST
DEPUIS   = FOR (= SINCE)

1. **Venir de**

English	French
Perfect tense ——————→	Present tense
Pluperfect tense ——————→	Imperfect tense

Examples

I **have just** eaten it	=	Je **viens de** le manger
I **had just** taken it	=	Je **venais de** le prendre

2. **Depuis**

English	French
Perfect tense ——————→	Present tense
Pluperfect tense ——————→	Imperfect tense

(a) **Perfect → Present**

How long **have** you been here?

= $\left.\begin{array}{l}\text{(Depuis quand} \\ \text{(Depuis combien de temps)}\end{array}\right\}$ êtes - vous ici?

I **have** been here for half an hour.
= Je **suis** ici depuis une demi-heure.

(b) **Pluperfect → Imperfect**

How long **had** you been waiting?

= $\begin{pmatrix} \text{Depuis quand} \\ \text{Depuis combien de temps} \end{pmatrix}$ **attendiez** - vous?

I **had** been waiting for 10 minutes.
= **J'attendais** depuis dix minutes.

§70. VOILÀ AND IL Y A

1. **Voilà** = $\begin{cases} \textit{there is} \\ \textit{there are} \end{cases}$ **when the object is visible.**

   e.g. Voilà un stylo!   = There's a pen!
         Voilà des pommes! = There are some apples!

   Note 1: Voici = here is or here are

   Note 2: Object Pronouns may be placed before Voilà and Voici.
              Me voici ! = Here **I** am !   **Le** voilà ! = There **he** is !

2. **Il y a** = $\begin{cases} \textit{there is} \\ \textit{there are} \end{cases}$ **when object not visible.**

   e.g. Il y a un stylo dans le tiroir = there is a pen in the drawer.

   Note 1: Il y a = ago   e.g. Il y a deux ans = 2 years ago.

   Note 2: Forms: il y a   il n'y a pas
                      = there is/are   = there isn't/aren't.

                      Y a-t-il?   N'y a-t-il pas?
                      = Is/are there?   Isn't/aren't there?

   Note 3:(With **en***)* il y en a   il n'y en a pas.
                      = there is/are some   there isn't/aren't any.

                      Y en a-t-il?   N'y en a-t-il pas?
                      = is/are there some? = Isn't/aren't there any?

§71. WEATHER

		Note the Imperfect
Quel temps fait-il?	= What's the weather like?	
Il fait beau	= It is fine	Il *faisait* beau
Il fait mauvais temps	= It is bad weather	,,
Il fait chaud	= warm	,,
Il fait froid	= cold	,,
Il fait du soleil	= sunny	,,
Il fait du vent	= windy	,,
Il fait du brouillard	= foggy	,,
Il pleut	= raining	Il *pleuvait*
Il neige	= snowing	Il *neigEait*
Il gèle	= freezing	Il *gelait*

Note: **par** un temps splendide = **in** fine weather.

Il fait jour	= It is light
Il fait nuit	= It is dark (i.e. night)
Il fait noir	= It is dark (= light off).

INDEX

The references are to page numbers

INDEX

INDEX